Una Mullally is an award-winning journalist with the *Irish Times*, author and broadcaster. She is the author of *In the Name of Love*, an oral history of the movement for marriage equality in Ireland. She lives in Dublin.

REPEAL THE 8TH

Edited by Una Mullally

Unbound

This edition first published in 2018

Unbound
6th Floor Mutual House, 70 Conduit Street, London W1S 2GF

www.unbound.com

Credits are continued on page 205.

Text Design by PDQ

A CIP record for this book is available from the British Library

ISBN 978-1-78352-516-4 (trade pbk)
ISBN 978-1-78352-517-1 (ebook)
ISBN 978-1-78352-449-5 (limited edition)

Printed in Great Britain by Clays Ltd, St Ive Plc

1 3 5 7 9 8 6 4 2

For all of the women who have travelled for abortions, for all of the women who couldn't afford to, for all of those who have told their stories, and for those who kept those stories to themselves, for all of those who are campaigning for women's reproductive rights in Ireland and Northern Ireland, and for those who have gone before us who did the same. For all of those who have suffered under the Eighth Amendment, our liberation is near.

Dear Reader,

The book you are holding came about in a rather different way to most others. It was funded directly by readers through a new website: Unbound. Unbound is the creation of three writers. We started the company because we believed there had to be a better deal for both writers and readers. On the Unbound website, authors share the ideas for the books they want to write directly with readers. If enough of you support the book by pledging for it in advance, we produce a beautifully bound special subscribers' edition and distribute a regular edition and ebook wherever books are sold, in shops and online.

This new way of publishing is actually a very old idea (Samuel Johnson funded his dictionary this way). We're just using the internet to build each writer a network of patrons. At the back of this book, you'll find the names of all the people who made it happen.

Publishing in this way means readers are no longer just passive consumers of the books they buy, and authors are free to write the books they really want. They get a much fairer return too – half the profits their books generate, rather than a tiny percentage of the cover price.

If you're not yet a subscriber, we hope that you'll want to join our publishing revolution and have your name listed in one of our books in the future. To get you started, here is a £5 discount on your first pledge. Just visit unbound.com, make your pledge and type **repeal5** in the promo code box when you check out.

Thank you for your support,

Dan, Justin and John
Founders, Unbound

CONTENTS

INTRODUCTION

UNA MULLALLY

In the midst of social change, what stories do we tell ourselves and each other? And do we remember them? Right now in Ireland, there are conflicting narratives about what kind of place we are and what kind of place we can be. What do we want to consign to the past and what do we want to preserve? What are we fighting for? The movement for women's reproductive rights in Ireland is a long and bitter one. It is also inspiring. Within that movement there are multiple narratives, but what is clear is that art, literature and design have emerged from the movement, and continue to do so. When this battle is over, that's a legacy worth preserving and reflecting on.

When social movements progress and realise their goals, what came before – the t-shirts, the badges, the essays, the poems, the placards – get put in drawers and in attics. No longer necessarily serving a purpose, the wave of art that pushed forward debate and stories and thoughts recedes. But this art is what colours a movement.

This book is an attempt to document the aspects of a movement that are often forgotten when its goal has been achieved. It is not a history of the movement for reproductive rights in Ireland, nor an academic study. It is not polemic nor a debate. What it does try to capture is the art, literature, design, personal experience, poetry and journalistic writing that have developed out of or been inspired by the movement for reproductive rights, particularly centring around the campaign

1

to remove the Eighth Amendment, the Irish constitutional ban on abortion.

In this book, you will find reflections from writers, artists, journalists, campaigners and people who have personally experienced, at a very visceral level, the impact of the abortion ban in Ireland, and also the thoughts and visual articulations of those who engage with the impact of those laws.

Our art and our conversations are products of our environment. The acts of expression related to our restrictive abortion laws at this time take many forms. They are murals on walls and ideas for poems; they are essays and personal stories; they are screenplays and short stories; they are textile designs and photography; they are graphic design and things we need to get off our chest. This collection of work is free-flowing, and purposefully chooses a thematic narrative over a linear one. The movement itself is both personal and collective political and social, and we discuss it with humour and with tears, anger and meditation. It is both abstract and concrete. As a result this anthology is purposefully inconclusive. It aims to both directly address the issues and reflect upon them.

It is difficult to have a perspective on something that is ongoing. But when civil rights campaigns achieve their goals, the narrative of their history always becomes a point of view. This book attempts to capture the energy, articulated through art and discourse as it happens. Some pieces directly address certain issues; others offer a broader assessment of our environment and social history.

Although the midst of progress can sometimes feel characterised by backlash, resistance and conflict, Ireland is experiencing a wave of social change that is driven by multiple generations; those who have stayed the course and fought for civil rights for decades, and a new generation agitating with righteous impatience for a country that reflects them.

Like many people, I was indoctrinated by the Catholic Church in school and at mass to believe that abortion was evil. As I grew older, the process of shedding that indoctrination was revelatory. My memories of how sex and reproduction were spoken about in school are hazy; visiting nuns talking about black marks on our souls, or equating our souls with the water used to clean our classroom paintbrushes – how one dirty brush could soil the whole jar. There were sensational lectures about abortion, using language I knew to be inflammatory, and later learned to be totally inaccurate. Sex was dangerous, to be feared, certainly not spoken about with adults beyond the classroom context of anatomical drawings of penises and wombs in biology books. The violent anti-choice language and imagery followed us around. It took up space on placards on Shop Street in Galway or outside the General Post Office in Dublin. I am thirty-four years old. This is not ancient history.

At sleepovers in friends' houses – sober, skittish ones first, then tipsy teenage ones – the secrets of families unravelled. We all had them; the older female relatives sent away to Magdalene Laundries, places for 'fallen women' or 'Mother and Baby Homes', or who had babies taken from them. Travel just a branch or less down the average Irish family tree, and you'll find these repeating patterns: the systematic imprisonment, punishment and forced exile of our own women; the illegal child trafficking; the abuse and torture. Occasionally the especially abhorrent, especially cruel, especially tragic stories make it into the headlines, but for every one of those, there are thousands more, the white noise of the subjugation and oppression of women.

The greatest oppression does not have to be meted out by some ferocious dictator. We do it to one another, to ourselves.

The collusion in how the bodies of Irish women have been policed – how lives have been destroyed, sometimes ended; how women in Ireland have been systematically punished for daring to be sexual beings – stinks of guilt and shame and secrecy.

Central to this grotesque misogyny and patriarchy has been the ultimate resistance to female independence and autonomy: denying women the right to decide when they want to reproduce, denying women birth control and access to abortion, and placing into the constitution articles that amplify a woman's 'life within the home' and a ban on abortion that equates a woman's life – a real, lived life – to that of 'the unborn'.

The State acknowledges the right to life of the unborn and, with due regard to the equal right to life of the mother, guarantees in its laws to respect, and as far as practicable, by its laws to defend and vindicate that right.

This is the Eighth Amendment, article 40.3.3. I was born in 1983, the year the Eighth Amendment was introduced to the constitution. Abortion had been illegal in Ireland since the foundation of the State, whereupon we adopted the British 1861 Offences Against the Person Act. In the 1960s, when abortion was legalised in Great Britain, Ireland lagged behind, the social backdrop – conservative lobbyists, a conservative society, and a then still strong Catholic Church – providing the momentum for a constitutional referendum to reinforce a ban on abortion that would be difficult to untangle.

One of the first times I voted was in another referendum on abortion, in 2002, which was an attempt to exclude the risk of suicide as grounds for abortion, and strengthen the constitutional ban on abortion. It was defeated.

The awakening of Irish generations is far more rapid now,

4

as information is more accessible and connections can be made with others who are fighting similar battles. Both inspired by and immersed in a new wave of feminism, as well as acutely aware of how progress made on women's rights continues to be reduced across the world, the movement for women's reproductive rights in Ireland has taken on an energy that is unstoppable.

This anthology is one part of a much larger canon. Not here are the countless other plays and poems and stories and performances and photographs, the private pieces of writing that no one will ever see, diary entries and letters to lovers and friends and family members, the words spoken late at night after a bottle of wine with friends. There are so many things unsaid. So many stories remain hidden in Ireland, swept under the carpet, nudged into the shadows, silenced out of shame and pain.

At the time of writing, Ireland continues to deny women living in the country, North and South, basic bodily autonomy, basic rights, basic healthcare. The art that has emerged from that denial is urgent and sad, it is poignant and pointed, but it tells a story that we can't forget, even after the Eighth Amendment is removed. This art is of us and speaks to us. It is both reflection and a rallying call. Its existence is necessary, but the goal is that it does not exist at all. For now, let's tell those stories.

A struggle is at its toughest when breakthroughs are imminent. It's often at that point that the most crucial art emerges. As this anthology shows, it takes many forms, but all of it is an expression of a time and a place. Our society and its faults inform our art and literature and conversations and thoughts. When we remember it and reflect on it, we are remembering an aspect of social history that will hopefully soon feel outdated, but today is the here and now.

A SHORT TIMELINE OF THE REPRODUCTIVE RIGHTS MOVEMENT IN IRELAND

1828 Offences Against the Person Act 1828
Section 13 laid out the death penalty for 'post-quickening' abortions.

1837 Offences Against the Person Act 1837
Section 6 made it an offence for 'pre- or 'post-quickening' (the moment in pregnancy when the pregnant woman feels foetal movements) terminations, but abolished the death penalty set out in the 1828 Act for abortion.

1861 Offences Against the Person Act 1861
Section 58 and 59 of the Act label procuring an abortion offence ('procure her own miscarriage'), and supplying instruments or poison for an abortion ('procure the miscarriage of any woman') an offence.

1935 Criminal Law Amendment Act 1935
Section 17 outlawed the sale, advertisement, importation etc, of contraceptives to Saorstát Eireann (the Irish Free State).

1945 Criminal Justice Act (Northern Ireland)
Section 25 criminalises abortion with the offence of 'child destruction'.

1968 The Abortion Act 1967 comes into effect
Legalises abortion in all of Great Britain, but not Northern Ireland.

1969 Fertility Guidance Company Ltd
The first 'family planning' clinic in Ireland was established in Dublin. It later became the Irish Family Planning Association.

1971 The Contraceptive Train
A group of Irish feminists travelled from Dublin Connolly train station to Belfast and back with contraceptives, challenging their illegalities in the Republic of Ireland.

1973 McGee v. Attorney General
A Supreme Court case which conferred a right to privacy in marital affairs. It was brought by Mary McGee, a woman who was instructed to use a diaphragm and spermicide as birth control, due to her endangering her own life should she get pregnant again (she had four children at the time). The Criminal Law Amendment Act 1935 prevented her from getting a prescription for birth control.

November 1980 The Health (Family Planning) Act 1979 comes into effect
Regulates the sale, importation and prescriptions for contraceptives: 'A registered medical practitioner may, for the purposes of this Act, give a prescription or authorisation for a contraceptive to a person if he is satisfied that the person is seeking the contraceptive, bona fide, for family planning purposes or for adequate medical reasons and in appropriate circumstances...'

19 March 1983 Sheila Hodgers dies
Hodgers, a woman from County Louth, died from cancer two days after giving birth to her third child. Following breast cancer surgery, while she was still taking medication, she became pregnant and stopped taking medication, as the medication could harm the foetus. She was refused painkillers and a caesarean section. She gave birth on 17 March and the baby died. Hodgers died two days later from multiple cancers.

September 1983 The Eighth Amendment referendum
A bitterly divisive referendum campaign concludes with a vote on introducing the Eighth Amendment into the Irish Constitution. The amendment confers equal right to life to a mother and a foetus. 66.9 per cent vote for the Eighth Amendment, 33.1 per cent against.

October 1983 The Eighth Amendment signed into law
Article 40.3.3 of the Constitution of Ireland read: 'The State acknowledges the right to life of the unborn and, with due regard to the equal right to life of the mother, guarantees in its laws to respect, and, as far as practicable, by its laws to defend and vindicate that right.'

January 1984 Ann Lovett dies
Lovett, a fifteen-year-old girl, died while giving birth beside a religious grotto in County Longford. Her baby also died.

1985 Condom sales liberalised
An amendment to the Health (Family Planning) (Amendment) Act 1985 allowed spermicides and condoms to be sold to people over eighteen without a prescription in certain outlets.

1988 SPUC v. family planning counsellors

The Society for the Protection of Unborn Children (SPUC) challenged Irish counselling agencies for providing women with information on how to communicate with abortion clinics abroad under Article 40.3.3. The High Court Case AG v. Open Door Counselling and Dublin Wellwoman Centre prevented those agencies from helping women by providing information about how to obtain an abortion abroad. SPUC also took cases against student unions doing the same.

1991 The IFPA fined for selling condoms at the Virgin Megastore record shop in Dublin

1992 The X Case

A landmark Irish Supreme Court case that established the right of Irish women to abortion if the life of the pregnant woman was at risk. The case involved a fourteen-year-old girl, known as 'X', who was raped by her neighbour and was suicidal. Before travelling for an abortion, the girl's family asked the Irish police (Garda Síochána) if DNA from the aborted foetus could be used as evidence in a court case against the neighbour who raped the girl. The Attorney General then sought and received an injunction against the girl travelling to have an abortion. This injunction, granted by the High Court, was appealed to the Supreme Court and overturned, establishing that a pregnant woman had a right to an abortion if there was a risk to her life, including suicide. The girl had a miscarriage shortly after the judgement was made.

November 1992, Three more referendums

Referendums are held on the Twelfth, Thirteenth and Fourteenth Amendments to the Constitution of Ireland. The Twelfth Amendment sought to state that the risk of suicide should not be a reason for a legal abortion. The Thirteenth Amendment addressed the freedom to travel out of the State, and that travelling for an abortion should not prohibit this freedom. The Fourteenth Amendment was about the right to distribute information about abortion services outside of Ireland. The Twelfth Amendment was rejected, the Thirteenth and Fourteenth passed.

The Thirteenth Amendment and the Fourteenth Amendment are inserted into the Constitution of Ireland as subsections of Article 40.3.3, regarding the right to travel for an abortion, and the right to receive information on abortion in other jurisdictions where terminations are legal, adding to Article 40.3.3.

'This subsection shall not limit freedom to travel between the State and another state.'

'This subsection shall not limit freedom to obtain or make available, in the State, subject to such conditions as may be laid down by law, information relating to services lawfully available in another state.'

1995 Regulation of Information (Services Outside the State For Termination of Pregnancies) Act
The act that governs how information about the availability of abortion outside of Ireland is made available.

March 2002 Another referendum
A referendum on the Twenty-fifth Amendment proposed again that suicide not be grounds for legal abortion in Ireland. The attempt to tighten Ireland's abortion laws further failed, with 50.42 per cent voting against and 49.58 per cent voting for.

2005 The IFPA sued the Irish government in the European Court of Human Rights
On the grounds of right to privacy on behalf of three women who were forced to travel outside of Ireland for terminations.

2010 The European Court of Human Rights found in favour of the IFPA
The European Court of Human Rights found the Irish government had violated the European Convention on Human Rights with regards to the IFPA's 2005 case and was ordered to pay damages.

July 2012 The Abortion Rights Campaign is founded
Initially named the Irish Choice Network

October 2012 First March for Choice
The first March for Choice organised by the Abortion Rights campaign is held in Dublin, leading to annual marches and simultaneous rallies and actions in cities all over the world over the next six years (at the time of writing).

October 2012 Savita Halappanavar dies
Halappanavar died in a hospital in County Galway after complications from a septic miscarriage. She asked for a termination, which was refused by the hospital. The baby was stillborn on 24 October. Halappanavar died 28 October.

January 2014 The Protection of Life During Pregnancy Act 2013 comes into effect
Allows for legal terminations where pregnancy endangers a woman's life, and repealing Sections 58 and 59 of the Offences Against the Person Act 1861.

2014 Ms Y
The story emerged of a young asylum seeker, Ms Y, who arrived in Ireland pregnant after being raped in her home country. Suicidal, she went on hunger strike. At twenty-five weeks pregnant she delivered a baby by caesarian section in August 2014.

December 2014 Miss P
A woman who was brain-dead after suffering head trauma, and who was eighteen weeks pregnant, was kept alive against her family's will until the High Court ruled that doctors could switch off her life support machine.

2015 Coalition to Repeal the Eighth Amendment
A coalition of groups to advocate for the repeal of the Eighth Amendment is founded, creating a growing alliance of over one hundred organisations.

April 2016
A twenty-one-year-old woman in Northern Ireland was given a suspended sentence when her housemates reported her to police after she used abortion pills bought online to induce a miscarriage.

June 2016 Repeal Project
The Repeal Project is founded by Anna Cosgrave, creating the iconic black and white sweaters. Several other pro-Repeal grassroots groups emerge including The HunReal Issues, Strike4Repeal, ROSA (for Reproduction rights, against Oppression, Sexism and Austerity) and more, continuing to build on activism for reproductive rights that has been ongoing for decades.

March 2017 Abortion pill raids
The Police Service of Northern Ireland (PSNI) raid premises, including a workshop of a pro-choice campaigner, on International Woman's Day, searching for abortion pills.

April 2017 Citizens' Assembly
The Citizens' Assembly, established to examine the issue of abortion laws and the Eighth Amendment and make recommendations to the Oireachtas, votes overwhelmingly that abortion access should not be regulated by the constitution and instead should be legislated for.

September 2017 Referendum on the horizon
The Taoiseach Leo Varadkar proposes that a referendum on the Eighth Amendment be held in May or June 2018.

Autumn 2017 Committee on the Eighth Amendment
A joint committee established by the Irish houses of parliament convenes to consider the recommendations of the Citizens' Assembly and to hear from experts on the issue, with a view to reporting to the Oireachtas regarding abortion and the constitution.

1

PERSONAL STORIES

Series of personal stories in collaboration with the X-ile Project and the Repeal Project.

ANONYMOUS

I have a child already, a beautiful, intelligent little girl who I would not give up for the world. I had her quite young, but abortion was never an option for me. She was mine and I loved her right from the first moment I knew I was pregnant. I want to get this across first, as I feel that people really don't understand that abortion is situational. This was my situation with my daughter but, sadly, situations change.

In December 2015 I discovered I was pregnant upon finishing a highly abusive relationship. I had been suffering from depression for three years preceding this and had got myself mixed up with a horrible man. My depression had led me to this situation; not thinking right, being with a man I shouldn't have been with and having unprotected sex. People can say women shouldn't get themselves pregnant and then they wouldn't need an abortion, but can a woman who is suffering from a mental illness really be held accountable? I think not. If I were living in a country that allowed abortion, I could have gone to a clinic and closed this chapter of my life safely and with dignity, but sadly I don't. In fact, because abortion is illegal, I am lucky to be still sitting here to tell my story.

Having got the positive result, I sought out options for abortion online. As a single parent I couldn't dream of having another child. It wasn't about me any more; it was now about my daughter, I couldn't allow her life to be changed so drastically because her mother had been careless. I went online and researched abortion, but it was too expensive for me to travel and I wouldn't be able to find the money. I did then what most girls do; I found an abortion-pill website. Over the coming days I spoke to the women there via email. They were very helpful and made the process so much easier. I thought I had found my solution; all I had to do was drive to Belfast, get the pills, take the first one and I would have ended this chapter in my life.

However, a week before the pills were due to arrive, I began to bleed. It wasn't much, just a small amount. I thought to myself it would just end the pregnancy and that would be that, so I ignored it. After a few days, though, I thought I may as well get a check-up. I knew I wasn't keeping the baby, but I still had another child to think about and I needed to be healthy. I booked an appointment with the local maternity service, told them I was around four to five weeks and had bleeding, and they booked me in for a scan on that basis.

There was nothing to see in the scan. The nurse quizzed me on dates, but all the bloods checked out – I was pregnant, but there was no baby to see.

After three internal scans and a lot of discomfort, I was told it was an ectopic pregnancy. The pregnancy hormone levels were still rising, which meant the foetus was still growing and my fallopian tube could rupture at any point. For this reason I was booked in for emergency surgery the same day. You can imagine my dismay at going in for a scan and ending up in an operating room, having never had an operation in my life. I underwent surgery that same day to remove my fallopian tube and the pregnancy on medical grounds, which is deemed appropriate in Ireland.

I know some hearing my story will think I got what I wanted – an abortion in Ireland that was deemed medically viable – but this certainly was not a dream situation for any woman to experience.

If I had not had the courage to go to the hospital and have myself looked at, I would have taken those pills and thought the abortion was complete, but the pregnancy would have continued to grow regardless. These tablets do not cover ectopic pregnancies, meaning I could have died from a ruptured fallopian tube and subsequent blood poisoning.

If abortion was legal I could have gone to an abortion clinic, been seen, told it was ectopic pregnancy and had everything treated right there and then. Instead I had to put my life on the line, completely unaware that the foetus growing inside me could kill me.

It angers me to think any woman will have to go through what I went through and maybe even worse. I am lucky to have escaped with my life. If I had made it to Belfast and taken those pills, who is to know what could have happened? I am so thankful I had enough courage to go to the maternity service and have it looked into, but who is to say another woman will be as lucky? Going to have a check-up with other expectant mothers joyfully rubbing their bumps while you sit there feeling like a fraud isn't exactly a thing many women seeking abortion will do. This is putting their health at risk, but the shame our society inflicts on women seeking abortion keeps them from having a check-up. I felt so embarrassed and ashamed as I waited to be seen, but am so thankful I did it.

My story is tough, as I got into it at a time when I wasn't thinking clearly, but what woman does think clearly when dealing with an unplanned pregnancy? This country is putting women's lives at risk by not allowing them proper healthcare when it comes to abortion. Things happen, mistakes happen, women should not have to suffer so much pain and mental torture to regain control of their bodies. Abortion is not for everyone, but no one should be denied the choice. It was once not for me, but when I truly needed this service, I wish it could have been something my country allowed me.

SARA FALKENSJO

I was twenty-seven. I was living in Ireland, and me and my boyfriend got pregnant. It wasn't planned at all. In fact, my doctor had told me that I might need to have hormones to get pregnant. I was kind of worried to tell my boyfriend, because we had never talked about what we would do if it happened, but he agreed with my decision to have an abortion and was supportive.

I would have done it in Ireland if it was available there, because the flight was very expensive. The procedure itself wasn't. It's not expensive in Sweden. My mom came with me and everyone was really nice. For me, having an abortion maybe wasn't as scary to someone who was Irish. There was no fear on my part whatsoever. I told my dad too. He was supportive, but he also knew there would be no point in not supporting me!

I don't think people should take the decision to have an abortion lightly, and it's a decision that affects you a lot, but it's something that should be available for everyone. The decision was something for me to make, not for society to make. If you don't feel like you're suited to be a parent, you should have a choice.

Sara Falkensjo, interviewed by Rosita Boland in an extract from an *Irish Times* article

HELEN LINEHAN

A couple of years ago, I exposed myself to the unsuspecting public. I'm really not the type to draw attention to myself, but this time, I felt I had to. I'm not embarrassed or regretful, although there are many people who would believe that I should be. Abortion is awful. Necessary and awful. It's like a riddle; something needed but never wanted. Nobody wants it. When I had mine, it was after the twelve-week scan. The radiologist detected a skeletal problem and after a more detailed internal scan, the diagnosis was very bad. I didn't know how lucky I was. Sounds weird, I know, but this was in the UK. I was treated with compassion and offered counselling after the pregnancy was terminated.

If I had been in Ireland, I would have had no option but to continue with the pregnancy despite knowing that while the baby would grow in my womb, it would not survive birth.

My husband and I shared our story with Amnesty's campaign to repeal the Eighth Amendment in Ireland to give women a choice and ultimately the rights over their own bodies.

I went on TV. I was at press conferences. I went on Channel 4 news with Cora Sherlock, an anti-choice campaigner. When I talked about my experience she said, 'But what about the baby?' I felt it was best not to engage with her.

I was ready for a backlash on Twitter and Facebook. Surprisingly, I had an overwhelming reaction of support and outrage that laws like the Eighth Amendment exist. Not many people knew about it. I also had many personal stories sent to me. I have some trolls. Some people find solace in sending me diagrams of the abortion procedure. Another stranger on Facebook asked me, 'Would you murder me, Helen?'

The problem is that nobody wants to talk about it, but it's here. It's always here. Whatever your beliefs, women always have and will continue to have abortions. Abortions for medical reasons or for unwanted pregnancies, women need this choice. I swear, if men could have babies, there'd be an abortion app.

I was a bit shy and embarrassed being on the news and telling my story to the press, but I'll never be embarrassed, regretful or ashamed of having an abortion and neither should anyone who has to go through it. For whatever reason.

LUCY WATMOUGH

In 2015, I was not raped. There was no foetal abnormality. My life was not at risk. I was just a girl who was not ready to be a mother. I cannot begin to explain the gut-wrenching fear that I felt in the office of my GP that day when I was told that I was, in fact, in no uncertain terms, pregnant.

The thought that I could be pregnant had never occurred to me in a million years. I had only had a very brief fling with the father, which was by no means anything even close to a relationship, and it was most certainly over. As I sit in that little office, I cannot comprehend what is happening – we had been careful. I was on the pill. I buy four pregnancy tests on the way home, unable to believe what I have just been told. Each little blue line that appears in the test window adds to the panic rising in my chest. I carry on with my day silently, telling only a close friend, who hugs me, again, silently.

My emotions are extremely mixed over the following two weeks, as I decide what I am going to do. I debate whether or not to tell the father, eventually deciding that it would be the best thing for both of us if he knew.

I cannot say that it is easy for me to decide, but ultimately I know that I am too young for motherhood, and nowhere near financially stable enough to provide for a child. I'm not one for gambling, and to take such a risk with another life feels irresponsible.

I decide that I want to have a surgical abortion – I want to just go in, get it over and done with and go home. Only three people know about the pregnancy, and carrying my secret around for weeks starts to tear me up. It's all I think about every day; from the moment I wake up to when I eventually manage to get to sleep at night.

I try to act normal around friends and family, attempting to hide my morning sickness so as not to arouse suspicion. At home, surrounded by people, I have never felt more scared or alone. The father and I speak regularly during this period, both of us terrified with our Big Secret. He offers multiple times to go with me to London, but I am adamant I want to go by myself, not feeling that this is an experience I want to share. I feel guilty enough having burdened him with this situation already.

When the day of the abortion finally arrives, I tell nobody that I am going. Sitting in Dublin airport on my own, I feel as if the eyes of everyone there are upon me, judging me. I remember shrinking into my chair as I waited at my gate, terrified that somebody would somehow know what I was going to do. The clinic I go to is in Brixton. A nurse takes me to a private consultation room, where she runs through some medical questions and performs a scan. In the waiting room there are two couples and three other women on their own. One of them is Irish, like me, which I notice as she whispers to the receptionist. It is the only noise in the room, as the rest of us sit in silence, waiting. As the nurse calls my name I dig my nails deeper into the palms of my hands and they bleed.

The room they lead me into feels very clinical and it smells like a dentist's office. I have opted for conscious sedation, as I'm flying back that evening. Lying on the bed I begin to feel woozy, but I am fully aware of what's happening to me. The procedure isn't pleasant – despite the drugs I find it painful and it feels extremely invasive. They dilate my cervix manually and then mash up my insides with a speculum, before hoovering my womb out. I discover that having my womb hoovered feels exactly like you would expect it to. The nurse holds my hand the entire time, reassuring me that it's almost over. The whole procedure takes about six minutes, although every minute feels like an hour as I wait for the doctor to remove his instruments from inside me. I close my eyes and bite my tongue the entire time, stopping myself from screaming 'GET OUT'. I just want everything and everyone to get out of me, and to go home to my own bed. But I'm not at home.

When it's over I'm taken into a recovery room, where I lie on a reclining chair as I wait for the wooziness to wear off. I'm given a cup of tea and a biscuit, which I consume as I try to ignore the raw feeling between my legs as pain settles into my uterus. There's a lady crying in the chair next to me. I wish I was at home. I wish I was not on my own. When I'm allowed to leave, I precariously make my way to Gatwick airport on public transport. Although upset and sore, I feel relieved, and set about taking my bruised and bloodied womb back across the Irish Sea.

I find the wait at the airport is the worst part of the entire thing. I curl up in a ball as the pain medication starts to wear off. A very kind lady notices me and helps me to the bathroom. She goes to the shop and gets me some ibuprofen and a drink. I cry quietly all the way back to Dublin.

By the time I get to arrivals I'm all over the place. I've felt myself unravelling the longer I'm away from home. The guy involved is collecting me and relief washes over me when I see him. It finally all feels over. He holds my hand in the taxi and we say nothing, not knowing what to say. I squeeze his hand a little tighter over every speed bump. I stay with him for two days and he looks after me as I get back to normal. The pain subdues but lasts for longer than I expected, but my happiness to no longer be pregnant overrides everything. I await the guilt that I've been told by society to expect, but it never arrives. In the end, I'm thankful for the choice I made. What's difficult is how alone my country has made me feel.

I didn't talk about my abortion for two months after I had it and it slowly started to drive me mad. I was so afraid of people finding out, of being judged for allowing myself to get pregnant in the first place; of being judged for not wanting my baby. My relationships with family and friends became strained as I dealt with something that they had no idea about. I broke down in tears in the kitchen one day in September, and told my mother what I'd been terrified she'd find out for months. All she did was hug me and reassure me that she supported my decision.

The more I talk about my abortion, the lighter I feel. The stigma put upon it in Ireland made the entire situation so much more difficult than it already was, as I felt my unwanted pregnancy was something to be ashamed of. Ireland's archaic abortion laws mean that thousands of women every year go through a similar ordeal to mine, and many live with it silently for the rest of their lives. Mothers, daughters, sisters, wives, friends. They're our bodies, and it's our choice.

Lucy Watmough, in conversation with Bárbara A. Soares
for *The Circular*

2

LAUNDRY

MARY COLL

My grandfather sent everything to the nuns
for a thorough cleaning,
including my mother,
fervently they washed away every stain.
Hold us up to the light,
and there is hardly a trace of me left in her,
or her left in me.
Things are forever getting separated in the wash,
a fawn silk stocking,
a tiny pink sock with no matcher,
the price to be paid for getting your laundry done.

Mary Coll is a Limerick poet and playwright.

3

THE QUESTION OF CONSENT
ANNE ENRIGHT

1. Pregnancy without consent

Sex without consent is a terrible thing, we know that. Why are we less shocked by pregnancy without consent? We understand the horror of rape – to have someone inside you for thirty seconds, or ten minutes, or repeatedly for hours, days, years, to enter your body without your joyful invitation, this is known to be a terrible violation, a breaking of the boundaries of the self, a trauma from which it is hard to heal.

We see the drama here. We imagine or remember the pain inflicted and the pleasure taken, and we condemn the act absolutely. But this drama is also a kind of distraction from an ethical argument that might be made about your body: who gets to use it and on what terms.

I am making this argument for the sake of argument, in a way – I think it extends the debate. I use the term 'pregnancy without consent' because it coincides with the Christian right's view that a conceived embryo is already, and instantly, a human being, and this view begs questions about what human beings can do to each other, and why.

What right does another human being have to be inside

your body for many months, to make their way out of your private parts in a bloody, difficult and painful way (to then turn to you for love, perhaps until the day you die?). What is the difference between this and rape – I mean, what is the exact difference? One is seen as sexual, though it is probably more about power; the other is seen as sacred, though it has its roots in a sexual act. They both happen in someone else's body. In the first, the question of consent is seen as key, in the second it is not.

In the nine-month occupation that is a pregnancy, the embryo has no agency, of course, and no intention to harm. But an absence of intention does not confer any rights. Just because someone does not mean to use you does not give them the right to use you. Does it? Or hurt you. The fact that an embryo cannot ask for consent does not mean that consent *must* be given. An embryo takes no pleasure from its presence in your body, but this does not give it ownership of your body any more than a grown man has ownership over your body's interior. The hidden fact in the Eighth Amendment is that the term 'unborn' does not mean 'human being', as the mother is a human being – if it did, then the mother's rights might also be asserted. The 'unborn' here is code for 'biology', 'happenstance' or 'life itself'.

It may be argued that when a woman consents to unprotected sex she is also consenting to pregnancy, but I do not know if you can make an agreement with someone who does not yet exist. The hidden power, in this contract with no one, lies not with the physically powerless embryo, or the legally powerless pregnant woman, it lies with the father, or with the father-as-state, who asserts control, from a sometimes indifferent distance, over both.

I know the word 'rape' is shocking in this context, but its

opposite word 'consent' is not so much shocking as clear. This argument may sound slightly absurd, not to mention harsh, but it is exactly as harsh and as absurd as the Eighth Amendment to the Irish constitution, which is widely understood without making any sense.

2. Women are very frightening

I do not know how many times people had unprotected sex in Ireland last year, but in 2016 there were 60,000 live births. Figures quoted in the *New York Times* estimate that 31 per cent of pregnancies end in miscarriage, which means that nearly 30,000 conceptions failed in Ireland last year due to natural causes. If all life is sacred, then all life did not get the memo.

Conservative figures, given by the Crisis Pregnancy Agency, say that 3,265 Irish women went to England or Wales to procure abortion in 2016, down over 50 per cent from a high of 6,673 in 2001. The biggest shift happened among women in their twenties (those born after the referendum of 1983), with numbers declining from 4,089 to 1,563, a reduction of over 60 per cent.

Pro-life campaigners don't seem to trust people much, though in my experience people do the best they can. Women especially are not to be trusted. Pro-life campaigners talk as though women are naturally opposed to the rights of 'the unborn'. But many women conceive by accident – some even against their wishes – and the babies they grow inside their bodies can be welcomed and much loved. Other babies, however, are born after long months of their mother's anguish and incomprehension that her body should be so used – and after her body, her life. Is this the way the pro-lifers think about their own mothers? That they have to be saved from her rage, her sense of life's unfairness, her murderous intent?

There is an overlap of nine months, when the smaller life depends on the bigger, and not the other way around. This is just true. If a foetus dies, the body surrounding it does not die, or not usually. The mother's life is the more powerful thing. This is very frightening, when you think about it. So, yes, women are very frightening, despite their almost universal willingness to please people, to smile and be nice.

3. The middle-class solution

Recently I spoke to a reasonable, sane, normal Irishwoman who said that she was against abortion, and because she was so reasonable, sane and normal, I was curious what she meant by that. Was she against the morning-after pill? Certainly not. What about chemical abortifacients? They did not really worry her too much. So, what about terminations before twelve or thirteen weeks, the time when woman are often given the all-clear to confirm their pregnancy to family and friends? This woman was not, being pretty sane, against terminations during this window, when pregnancy is not considered medically certain. She was also, just to make it clear, in favour of abortion in cases of fatal foetal abnormality, rape and incest. Many bases were covered, in other words. In 1983 this woman might have voted 'against abortion', despite the fact that she is not against abortion, especially during those weeks when the natural loss of an embryo is called 'miscarriage'. If she was asked to vote for or against 'assisted miscarriage', there is a chance that she would tick a different box.

Hers is perhaps a middle-class form of denial, being pragmatic, compassionate and a little bit pious. You could say that travelling to England is also a middle-class solution: it depends on people having literacy skills, credit cards, supportive parents if needs be, an amount of spare cash. It is not a solution for people in denial about what has happened to them – the girl raped by her stepfather, for example, who can tell no one, so deeply does she absorb his projected shame. But for many women 'assisted miscarriage' is a reasonable solution to an overwhelming problem, and had the vote not happened in 1983, it might well be available now, in the way that the morning-after pill is legally available and widely used.

4. America

Many of the women – especially Catholic women – who voted for Donald Trump were also against abortion and assumed, in a slightly unreal way, that Trump agreed with them (to be fair, it is not clear from any of his comments that Trump knows the connection between grabbing someone by the pussy and making them pregnant).

We live in an age of symbols. In 2016, people in Britain and the USA voted for the tribal and the irrational when they went for Brexit and for Trump. We know something about all this in Ireland because we had a tribal, symbolic vote in 1983. We've seen the cruelty of that symbolic choice play out in our hospitals, and our airports, and our lives for over thirty years. We know how debilitating it is to argue with the religious right and how wounding it is to face down their trolls.

If we, in Ireland, can repeal the Eighth Amendment, that shift will echo around the world. It will be heard in El Salvador, where women are imprisoned for the natural loss of their babies; it will be heard in those Australian states where abortion is both available and illegal at the same time; it will be heard in Poland, where 30,000 people marched against the further restriction of abortion laws, and won. It will be heard in America where, state by state, the rights conferred by Roe v. Wade are being whittled away, to the especial detriment of poor women, who own little or nothing, not even the body in which they walk around.

The message is not just about women's right to choose, it is about how countries work. Democracies must also be allowed to change.

Anne Enright is the author of *Making Babies*, a book of essays about motherhood. Winner of the Man Booker Prize, her work is translated into more than forty languages.

4

WHAT IS A WOMAN?
AISLING BEA

Excuse me, madam. What the hell is a 'Woman'?
Why, thank you for your question, sirmadam.

A Woman (plural 'Women'?):
The Oxford English dictionary describes Woman as '*neither fruit, nor vegetable, but something in between, like a cucumber or a peanut*'.

William Shakespeare described Woman as '*a giant pain in the hole and the reason I didn't become a farmer*'.

John Keats described Woman as '*like… a really nice plant pot*'.

And Homer described Woman as '*D'oh!*'.

Anthropologist Britney Spears described the middle-growth 'girl-Woman' stage as 'not a girl, not yet a Woman' – this is the stage up to and around the twenty-five-year mark, just before Woman's album sales start dwindling and their emotional support network and cash runs out.

You may know Women from having seen them on documentaries on the television; you may have even been lucky enough to see one scampering across the road at night, or rooting through bins for the remnants of some discarded kebab, or if you managed to look behind you while you were being born, there would have been a big giant sweaty one right there.

What does a Woman look like? What is the terminology? Do they have any distinguishing features to look out for?
Well, this is a tricky thing. Women are innately shifty creatures, coming in many shapes and forms. They can be big as a man or small as a boy. Woman is so complicated in its make-up that despite all the magic in the world, the Dalai Lama has never been able to reincarnate himself into one, just into men.

Women come in many colours – black, white, brown, yellow, red when hot, blue when cold, green when sick, multicoloured when unwell and orange when on a night out. In some countries they even come in *invisible*. They cannot be seen or heard but you might feel one brush past you. In these countries, Women are so invisible that it is hard to tell whether the dishes and cutlery were moved by a Woman or a poltergeist. You can tell the difference because poltergeists are less angry and never have to clean up dishes.

You find Women versions in most of the animal kingdoms except for worms, sea stars and fungi (ironic, because in the human world, a *fun guy* is one who mates with lots of Women – this is a great joke, try it out at parties). These species do not have separate genders because they do not have enough banter to do well on the dating scene. Their pups are called 'girls' and resemble tiny, penisless men.

The weirdest thing about Women is that they all come from literally *inside* other Women, which is frankly... disgusting and unnatural.

Men also come from literally inside Women, which is still

weird and not the best way to go about things, because they are coming out of somewhere their penises have been growing for nine months, so when they are born, they're literally motherfuckers.

'Bras' are what Women use to store their obese man boobs in. 'Bras' are like soft milk-bottle tops. As soon as you take off a bra, fresh milk comes out. This is the only animal byproduct suitable for vegans.

A 'feminist' can be male or female and is a left-leaning fraud and wacko.

Other than a lack of scrotums, are there any differences between men and these Women?
Men are danglier down below and have shorter fingernails to prevent them scratching themselves to death.

To go to the toilet, Woman cannot do it the normal way – by holding her penis in her hand and shaking it until all the liquid is out. Woman must take her penis to a private bowl, connected to a hole in the floor on which she sits. Woman then hopes and dreams for a white knight to come and save her, says a little prayer and ALLLAZAZOOOO! – God takes all of the excess liquid and remains of the dainty nibbles that she has shared with her friends that day at brunch and makes them disappear.

As a man, the worst thing is to be accused of doing something *'like a Woman'*. Doing something *'like a Woman'* is a euphemism for doing something to an abysmal degree of absolute shiteness. Instead of saying that you did something like throwing, running or behaving *'not very well'* in your everyday language, you can handily use *'like a Woman'* or, if you are pressed for time, *'gay'* instead.

This is actually great, because it gives gay people and Women people a real boost to get a shout-out or mention. It has absolutely no negative effect on them whatsoever, especially the young gay people or Women people, who are too stupid to be affected.

A man can be accused of '*acting like a Woman*' if they engage in certain activities like '*sewing*' or '*cooking*', unless they become successful professionals at those things and then they are called '*tailors*' and '*chefs*'.

Women are more likely to be killed by men for being annoying than kill themselves. Men, especially those under fifty, are rarely killed by Women, but are most likely be killed by themselves. This is because talking about their feelings in their earlier years and learning coping language is a classic Woman thing to do.

Women are known to speak 66 per cent more than men. They are not classically trained to keep all the words inside their heads silently until they have a breakdown in their thirties like men are trained to do, which is a much classier way of behaving than the mad carry-on of Woman who lets her feelings leak out like air out of a radiator. Let us once again stress that doing anything '*like a Woman*', especially talking about feelings, is absolutely fucking disgusting and must not be encouraged at all.

Women get their word count up so high because, owing to their silliness, they have to repeat themselves a lot. They are not to be taken seriously when speaking and this is fair enough, because they are less important and as minorities only represent 51 per cent of the population. Understandably, men, who are often in a rush, forget they are there and have no time, because they are in a rush, to be conscious of them. They are too busy selecting ties for their next business meeting. The wrong tie could ruin a good deal.

Women also repeat themselves because the first time round, they are trying to make men do something boring and trying to ruin the fun. Women love having to repeat themselves as it gives them something to do during the day instead of just sitting on a cushion and staring out the window. Men call '*having to be reminded to do something that they did not do despite agreeing to do and it would really be nice if they did do it*', 'nagging'. This is not to be confused with the celebrated dating aid 'negging', where males are encouraged to be mean to Woman, thereby lowering her sense of self and confidence in order to flirt with her for twenty minutes to an hour in a bar. 'Negging' is a great way to catch a Woman. Lowering their self-esteem dries out their natural oils and makes them 45 per cent less slippery.

Then the males are able to comfortably swoop in and take advantage of her at her lowest and potentially marry her, which is a very exciting prospect/end goal for the recently soul-destroyed Woman.

No one can imagine Woman running the world, because they will get a period during an important meeting about the economy and bleed all over the expensive government chairs. Worst of all, they will cry if someone dies – a sign of weakness, which is unnatural and cannot be encouraged, because: Jesus, what next? Crying is only to be used when a sports team – which has done very badly for years but has worked really hard with a new energy and manager, and has very loyal fans – makes it to the final of the sporting event. Otherwise, face-leaking is an overreaction.

A friendship with Woman is well known to be a waste of time and dangerous – they could try and make you have a meat-free lunch with them. Vegetarian Women are known as 'lesbians' and if you ever see a vegetarian 'man', he is also a lesbian and is probably having sexual relations with Women too.

Numbers and stats
Statistically, Women can be affected by war, but statistically, never start them.

Women do and enjoy the following things: singing or not singing, dancing or not dancing, eating or not eating, wearing clothes, liking and disliking clothes, friendship, looking well, not giving a shit what they look like, giving a shit what they look like, community, working and not working, equal rights, shoes, not shoes, not being hurt and *The Great British Bake Off*.

Contrary to science websites like www.uni-ladmag.com and www.whenisitinternationalMENSday.com and lazy stand-up comedy, the above traits affect Woman's IQ and ability to perform mental arithmetic and park a car. The fact that only one Woman has ever won the prestigious Field Medal for arithmetic was not to do a failure in the education system or a lack of cultural encouragement and support for Women in these fields, because they are encouraged by society to do loads of counting every day – for things like calories, and days until their wedding. So they must just be stupider in their head brains.

Words that get Women into trouble: 'vagina', 'period', 'smear test', 'clitoris', 'abortion'. These medical terms are rightly deemed too **YUCKY YUCK YUCK** for people to say. 'Penis', 'testicles', 'sperm', 'vasectomy' and 'semen', however, are lovely and funny and can be said on television in front of children.

Women cannot be priests because they have never done anything cool enough. Jesus was able to turn one drink into another type of drink at a wedding, but all Woman can do is make blood, life, milk, piss, spit, tears and shit without dying – sometimes all at the same time. Nearly all Women can do this, so it is not special.

No Woman has ever walked on the moon, because:

'I have too much shit going on down here on earth, also I'm not arsed and also what would I WEAR?' – *official quote from Women.*

There would also be a risk that gravity would yoink the tampon out of Woman when she was floating around and she would get bloodstains all over the bright, white, shiny moon.

Women who don't smile at road workers or builders as they pass them en route to work in the morning are a particular brand of devil-worshipper that deserve everything they get.

Recently in Turkey, Women were advised not to laugh in public. This was at first seen as '*a violation of human rights*', but is now known to be a good thing, as it could have distracted cyclists.

We have been informed by reliable sources of 'everyone everywhere', that men are intimidated by funny Women. Women are intimidated by men, because men can kill Women with their bare hands.

Not having a witty, one-up reply to a Woman's joke is a terrifying thought. All men should be vigilant when walking home alone at night, in case a Woman jumps out of a hedge and tries some new material on them – the only thing the man can do to respond is strangle the Woman in self-defence. This will, statistically, go unpunished by the law. Please, please be vigilant and spread the word amongst the men community.

They say that in most cities, you are never more than six feet away from a rat or a Woman, or less than three feet if you are close to somewhere that serves food.

Tips
What to do if you find a Woman in your house
1. Do not panic. They are more afraid of you than you are of them, unless they are one of those bloody feminist ones.
2. You may not need to call the police. If you are fast enough, place a glass over the Woman, almost like a ceiling, then try to find how she got in. Many use doors, but some do

use windows. Block them up, because it is rare to just find one Woman; they normally come in packs. Once one gets in, the likelihood is that they'll all want to come in and that will ruin everything for everyone.

3. If you know they are there but cannot see them, you can draw them out with tiny bits of chocolate, a cheese board, a promise of money, equal rights or a month of free Netflix.

4. Now, some people don't mind having Women in the house; they positively like them and see it as more natural for them to be there running around than not. This is cool, but if you do keep one, make sure to be kind to it, keep it fed, watered, safe and warm, particularly during the winter, when they like to sleep more.

5. Women are like dogs in that they are loyal and can be man's best friend if you treat them right, but if you don't, they will bite your fucking face off.

6. Ways in which they are not like dogs is that they are not dogs.

If you are fascinated by Women and want to see more, there are Women zoos in most cities. This is great fun.

Some Women zoos are called '*strip clubs*' and, for a small fee, you can go with your friends and see Women perform tricks and even balance balls on their noses. Unlike with goats and sheep, you will have to pay more to pet them, even if you have already paid to look at them.

You will also often hear that Women aren't funny.

This is true.

· ·

Sirmadam: Thanks for this, but one more question 'how many "Women" will I need to change the lightbulb?'.

Me: I am sorry sir, I cannot answer this question, I earn too much money from my work in comedy and pay a handy man to do it for me.

Aisling Bea is an award-winning comedian, writer and actor.

5

ABORTION, REGRET AND CHOICE

KITTY HOLLAND

I've had two abortions – one in my twenties, about which I had no regrets. And one in my thirties, which I regretted deeply. It was from the latter I learned most about choice.

I wrote, in passing, about them in a column for the *Irish Times*, published in May 2017. Though I had not intended it to, it upset many.

I had not intended to 'come out' about my abortions (though I had, several years previously, considered it with a view to writing about how complex a choice having an abortion is, comparing and contrasting my experiences. I was dissuaded from doing so by an editor who felt at the time that it could compromise my perceived objectivity on the abortion issue. How far we have travelled that in Ireland 2017 revealing you have had an abortion is no longer seen as an ideological standpoint, but rather a fact of one's life).

I had to now, not because my abortions were important to share – though I do believe the more women talk of their abortion experiences, the more we will all see how commonplace unwanted pregnancies are in Irish women's lives – but because I knew I could not point out how lucky we Irish women who can choose to travel for abortion are, if I did not acknowledge my privilege.

The piece I wrote came eventually in response to a fundraising concert for the Repeal campaign, which I paid €32 to attend and which I enjoyed and was glad I chose to go to. I asked in the piece what, and who, the wider Repeal campaign was for. I asked as someone not involved in the campaign, but as someone observing and following it, what the campaign was really demanding.

What do we mean by women's equality? ... The right to choose what? Abortion? No. Accessible abortion is fundamentally not about being able to choose abortion.

It is about a woman who becomes unexpectedly pregnant being empowered to regain control of her body, to be able to make choices about her life – her education, her career, how many children she can afford, how many children she wants, if any.

Accessible abortion is essential if women are to achieve economic and political equality with men, and it is absolutely essential if the poorest, most marginalised women are to achieve economic and political equality with their middle-class sisters.

In truth, abortion is as accessible to most Irish middle-class women, like me, as it is to women in the Scottish Highlands or the Welsh valleys.

I have, however, interviewed many women – on Traveller sites, in direct provision centres, in emergency housing, in homes with little furniture, minimal food and no heating – who couldn't afford to spare €4 for a child's school trip, much less spend €32 on a concert ticket, or €500 on an abortion.

The Repeal campaign is on the cusp of a historic breakthrough for Irish women – a cause for huge celebration.

Sadly, dominated by middle-class identity politics, it has lost an opportunity to build an all-embracing feminist movement that could challenge the most persistent and damaging inequality for Irish women – economic inequality.

I knew the piece would touch raw nerves. I had, as an outsider, observed an abortion rights campaign, particularly since the death of Savita Halappanavar[1] in October 2012, grow in momentum and confidence. The right to choose, the right to not to have to travel, the right to decided what happens with one's body, as a woman or girl, without State or Church interference – all of these were well-articulated arguments, being made increasingly loudly, vociferously, irresistibly.

I had not, however – and forgive me if I was not listening well enough – heard enunciated the reasons women choose abortion; how fundamental, everyday, even perhaps boring – and deeply personal – these reasons are, and how if one cannot act on the choice of abortion, how deeply fundamental, everyday and certainly violating that will be to a woman or girl's very being. Nor had I heard, as centrally as I felt one should, how it is the poorest and most marginalised women in Ireland who are so violated.

In short, I was tired of hearing over and over of how this was a women's issue, but too little of how it was an essentially human, and in Ireland, a class issue.

Choice itself – whether it's about what housing we have, where our kids go to school, whether we choose health insurance or cannot, whether or not we can have an abortion – is a class issue. Our very capacity to fully own and inhabit our humanity is a class issue.

---

[1] Savita Halappanavar died in a Galway hospital in October 2012 after being refused an abortion while suffering from complications of a septic miscarriage.

Even getting it wrong, and making the wrong choice, is a privilege, and a class issue.

As said, I had two.

The first was when I was twenty-seven. I was on the pill – it failed – and when I got pregnant I was with a man whom I had been with for a little over a year. The relationship was clearly coming to an end. I was a freelance journalist. I knew my work and income were too precarious and yes, I wanted to do really well in my work. I wanted to focus on it. I was only starting out in journalism and it was important to me. I did not want to have a baby.

I told two other people I planned to travel to London for an abortion: my friend Mary, and my mother. Though my mother, telling me I was a 'fine age' to have a baby, said she would support me choice either way, I was in no doubt. It was an anxious time nonetheless.

I knew Marie Stopes, which had a branch in Dublin, provided abortion services in England. I made an appointment to see a counsellor there, who talked me through the options, including parenting, adoption and abortion. But we knew why I was there and she moved quickly to providing the information I wanted, including the Brixton clinic's number, which tube station to get off at and a map of the area with the clinic marked, and the necessary referral letter to say I had had pre-abortion counselling.

I made an appointment for the abortion for the following week, for a Friday so I could tell work I was 'going to London for the weekend'. One of the news editors commented, 'Isn't it well for you, skitting off to London for a few days.' I smiled back. What could I say?

At Dublin airport, as he dropped me off (I wanted to travel

on my own and get it done without fuss), the man told me if I changed my mind he'd be OK with it. I knew I wouldn't. A friend, Janet, met me at Gatwick and we went for dinner at an Italian restaurant, where I remember us having seafood pasta.

I stayed with Janet and she came with me to the clinic the following morning, having taken a day off from her new job in television. My appointment was for 8 a.m. and I had had to fast from midnight. Janet waited with me until I was admitted and we said our goodbyes.

I had a scan to determine the gestation. I was six weeks pregnant. Bloods were taken. I was weighed. I was asked to change into a surgical gown and was brought down to theatre.

My legs were put in stirrups in a chair similar to one you'd sit in at the dentist, and I lay back. As I was given the full anaesthetic, I remember thinking it all a bit surreal. *Am I really doing this?* I thought. *Me?*

I should probably be upset or scared, I thought, but I felt nothing.

I woke back in the ward, where there were four other women. One was a young woman, in her twenties I think, from Cavan, a county in Ireland. Another, English, had come into contact with chickenpox or measles during her planned pregnancy and was advised to terminate. Another, a young Asian woman lying on her bed behind her curtain, cried quietly.

I remember sitting at a table in the centre of the ward for a supper of battered fish and peas. I think there was a television and *Coronation Street* was on. And then we went to bed.

The following morning we were discharged early, about 8 a.m. I walked with the young woman from Cavan to Brixton tube station. She hadn't told her boyfriend she was having an abortion. 'He'd have had me down the aisle in ten minutes if he'd known I was pregnant,' she said.

We got to the tube station and parted company. I went out to Gatwick and mum called me while I was in WH Smiths.

'How are you feeling?' she asked.

'Just fine,' I said.

I had a daughter, Rosie, three years later. I knew without a doubt that I wanted a baby and I was able to choose to keep her, knowing I could provide a good life for her. I didn't stay with her father, though we remain friends.

Aged thirty-six, I was happy with my lot. Work was going well. I was now a staff reporter and I was in a good relationship. Unexpectedly, I became pregnant. Again, I had been using contraception, but I think a bad stomach bug with vomiting and diarrhoea caused it to fail. I didn't want another child, I thought.

And yet, I was thirty-six. If I didn't have this one, would I have another chance? Did I want another?

I went for crisis pregnancy counselling at the Well Woman Centre in Baggot Street in Dublin. This time neither I nor the counsellor, Michelle, knew what I wanted – though on some level, I did.

She told me to really, really think about it.

'Go and spend time on your own. Look at the skies, look at the stars. Think about the magnitude of this decision for you, and how insignificant it is really, to everyone else in the world.'

At the end of the day, she said, no one would really care what I chose to do. At the end of the day this was *my* decision and no one else's.

I think, given the legal requirement that crisis-pregnancy counselling be non-directional in Ireland, she went as far as she could to direct me away from abortion. She asked about the death of my mother four years earlier, and other sadnesses in my life that could be triggering my current emotional uncertainty.

'Don't make the wrong decision for you,' she said, as she nonetheless provided me with information on clinics in the Netherlands.

What did I want? I had no clear idea, or at least I couldn't articulate it to myself with any confidence.

I talked about it with my partner. He didn't want a child and had always understood I didn't want another. That's what I had always said. Why was I thinking about it now? Things were great the way they were.

But maybe I actually I did want another child. I have always loved babies. Maybe it would be nice for Rosie. Or maybe it would be really unsettling. Maybe, I thought, I could plan another pregnancy, in a year. I just wasn't ready for this now. But what difference would waiting fifty-two weeks make? It would give me time. But what did I need time for? I realised I did want another child.

It was agony. I couldn't think about anything else. I couldn't sleep. I couldn't focus on anything. I rang the clinic in Amsterdam, which the counsellor had said was better, gentler, than England. Cheaper, too.

I made an appointment but didn't book a flight. When I finally went to book the flight the prices were astronomical. I rang the clinic again and changed to a later date. This was messing now. This was crazy. I just wanted it over – the worrying, the ruminating, the not knowing what to do – for myself, for my eight-year old daughter, for work, for my relationship. It was all too much for me to decide on my own. I wanted someone else to tell me what to do. But this was my decision.

In the end I travelled. Again alone, wanting to 'get it over' without fuss. I was full of doubts on the flight, full of doubts on the train from Schipol airport. Full of doubts in the clinic. I kept pushing the doubts down. Stop thinking about them. Get it done.

The nurse who scanned me – again six weeks' pregnant – asked if I wanted more children. Yes, I said, just not now. She looked at me, reminded me of my age – thirty-six. I was determined not to be put off. Get it done.

Again, I was brought to theatre, my legs were put in stirrups and I lay back. Just a local anaesthetic this time and the woman doctor talked to me as she performed the abortion. It took maybe five minutes and was very painful. Get it done.

As with the first, ten years earlier, I felt huge relief when it was over. I even felt proud of myself, travelling home to Dublin. I had overcome all my fears. I had got through it, and got it done.

Now I would get back to normal.

Two or three days passed. All I felt was a huge, tear-filled sadness. It was over, but what had I done?

I remember crying on my bike on the way to work, wiping my face clean when I got there. I couldn't concentrate in work. I'd leave my desk and go to the bathroom to cry. There was one colleague I wanted to tell, but when I needed to most, she seemed to be having a day off. I got on with it. My work suffered.

I would cry when driving with my daughter to school, she in the back seat so she couldn't see the tears streaming down my face. I didn't want to see friends. I couldn't. I'd have to explain I was heartbroken, that I had caused it, and nothing – least of all me – made any sense.

In work, the then features editor, Miriam Donohoe, pulled me up on how I was failing to deliver, particularly on one project she wanted me to work on, and I had done nothing about. I had to walk away from her as she upbraided me, tears welling again.

I sent her an email telling her what had happened, how sad I was and how I was sorry, but I was finding it really hard to function. She was hugely supportive.

I didn't tell anyone else in work. I told perhaps two friends –

some weeks after the fact. I was so ashamed of myself. Not only was there the 'shame' of having had an abortion but there was the shame, too, of regretting it. I had let myself down, with aplomb, and I had only myself to blame. What a mess. What a self-inflicted mess.

I went back to Michelle.

As soon as I came into her room, she looked at me and sighed: 'You did it?' She handed me a box of tissues as I sat down. 'Here we go,' she seemed to say.

I saw her weekly for about three months. I was having 'post-termination-of-pregnancy' counselling – PTOP counselling. It has a name. It's clearly needed. It is free, funded by the Health Service Executive, and probably saved me from a breakdown.

Michelle and I talked about why I had had the abortion; about why I would inflict something of such personal and negative enormity on myself, knowing in my heart I did not want it, because I thought it was what other people needed or wanted, and that seemed more important.

Why had I so violently repressed my needs? Why had I ignored, isolated and hurt myself? Why had I been so horrible to me? Why, in fact, had I thought so little of myself that what I knew I needed, on a primal level, did not matter?

Why did I think I had no choice?

I spent those months, and since, thinking about how we women, from girlhood, are taught to think about others' needs, to care and share and never be selfish. These are good lessons, of course, but I believe, as we grow into women, we are taught to care too much about how others are, how others think of us – to worry deeply about how we look, how we are seen, how kind and caring and giving and selfless we are.

I thought about how women of all classes are taught to accept that our ambitions just might not be fully realised because others' – men's? – ambitions are possibly more important than ours; how perhaps we are better than men at fulfilling a caring role – running a family – and that is really what we want. Or should want.

And how, when we accept that our needs should not come first, we cause ourselves – not others – harm and pain.

I learned – radically it seemed – about caring about myself, about really listening to myself and, if necessary, taking time out to hear myself.

I learned about being kind to myself, forgiving myself for making such a mess of things, and recognising I really had been trying to do what I thought was best at the time.

I began to find it easier to be me, because being me had become really hard.

Most radically of all, I realised that what I need (and want) will always be more important to me than it is to anyone else, that only I can really know my needs and that in fact what other people think about my wants and my needs really doesn't matter.

Ultimately I 'cured' myself by choosing to have another baby. My son, Alfie, was born about two years later.

I know some will find this difficult to read. Some who are anti-abortion, or who cannot have a baby, or who could not travel when they needed to might recoil from this account of my abortion crisis. Some who are pro-choice might feel uncomfortable with my tale of abortion regret.

I cannot change that, but I can share what I know these experiences showed me – the importance of choice.

I have had two happy pregnancies. Both were overwhelmingly emotionally positive experiences – from reading week-by-week details in *What to Expect When You're Expecting*, to bursting to tell people, being careful about what I ate, thinking up baby names and looking forward to the next scan. I loved the first waves of movement, progressing to little kicks beneath my swelling belly. I was excitedly, happily consumed with it all.

And I have had two crisis pregnancies, the second the inverse of all the above – overwhelming anxiety as the days flicked by and the crisis progressed, the panic about getting clinics and flights booked, desperately not wanting to talk about it, dreading that anyone might find out, hating the situation I was in, consumed with stress and worry, wanting it over.

No one knows what either feels like unless they have been through it. And every woman's experience of pregnancy has been and will be unique – our emotions, hopes, fears, anxieties, wants and needs. They are ours. Ours. Only we women – the ones who 'do' pregnancy – know what they are, and what, in their experiencing, is right for us.

I know this because I got it wrong once. I made the wrong choice, believing perhaps I could weigh and analyse the pros and cons, like some kind of intellectual checklist, and impose a logic, or a sense of the 'right thing to do' from outside of me, on what to do about a procedure that in the end would be experienced only by me.

The capacity to exercise choice is fundamental to our humanity. To make the right choice is human, and to err is human. When that is circumscribed, or worse, denied because of our gender or our class, our very humanity is limited.

I wrote the *Irish Times* column because I felt that privilege keenly, and wasn't hearing it from the campaign.

Kitty Holland is social affairs correspondent for the *Irish Times*. In 2012 she broke the story of the death of Savita Halappanavar in Galway University Hospital in October of that year, and has written extensively on abortion.

6

HISTORY LESSON
ELAINE FEENEY

The Stone Age began around 10,000 years before Jesus came
*   and made the Christians.*
There were others too. Gods. Ages. Stones.

In 2010, a man tells me I shouldn't be wearing purple tights if
    I want to be middle management.

It's all about impressions and right now you're giving off a purple
*   kind of flowery one.*
Same with tattoos and piercings. Rotten teeth.

I keep the purple tights on my curved legs. I have no
    rotten teeth.
He keeps power. Mostly in his pants. He has a mouth
    of silver fillings.

My mother was born in a three-bedroom terrace in 1955.
She wanted to be the cowboy with a cap gun on the street,
Christmas Day.
She wasn't mad about the *injians*.

She never knew her history and it drives her mad.
She's a furious reader.
Taught me to be a furious reader. Read us endless stories.
Even stories that matched our birth dates.
They were my favourite. Her voice growing tired.

People began to farm and lay down roots and make cheese and
they say the first farm men were very clever men,
knew how to balance staying beside the sea and not getting wet.

My Nana brings digestive biscuits into the
London air-raid shelter night after night.
Somewhere near St Thomas's, she said.
She calls her first son Thomas. My Dad.
He teaches me three things;

always drive into skid marks on an icy road.
He is the most important person in the world.
And when I'm not a cunt, I'm not too bad at all.
Honestly. All things considered.

Nana is glad of the break from slopping out the shit buckets
    in the hospital.
She's not a hundred per cent sure who's dropping bombs
    on her,
but she likes the evening company. They sing songs.
    She loves to sing.

Her mother died when she was four from a burst appendix.
She's never been very sure of anything since except how
    she loves to sing.

And how very very tall and very handsome her father was.
She liked to drink brandy and smoke the odd cigarette.

I spent one full hour convincing some friends that women
    said poems in Ireland before
Eavan Boland. The women friends are suspicious.
    They have English degrees.

It's difficult to remember who first sailed around the
    Cape of Good Hope,
or of Storms, Dias or da Gama? But man's stealing stuff
    takes a Frankensteinian turn.
Or at least now some ass is keeping a logbook of all the
    bastarding things they can do to others.

This would appear to be a good thing.
Silk and spice being basic human needs,
like diamonds and bread and the internet and hoarding.

We can say for sure that Magellan proved the world was round
    even if;

a woman is lying under a sycamore tree
and watches a dappled grey horse gallop towards her,
steely long legs appear all of a shot, not making sense,
she is a long time pregnant, her nipples thick and dark.
Soon she will give birth, she knows the earth is round
as she sees the horse over her large belly.
It is all too sudden. It must be a ball.

And besides, Magellan died through his experiment.
But this is just a technicality.

57

She keeps this information to herself.
She doesn't believe in the many of their any gods.
And besides, she doesn't want to die for knowing stuff.

Christopher Columbus was a great man.

In the small salmon bedroom of her terrace house,
they put chloroform over my other Nana's nose on one
    of her eleven labours.
This child survives. She's thankful for not losing another child.
Do your duty. You must do your duty.
It is sometime in the 60s, she's not too sure. She was
    collapsed, she tells me.

Skip through Martin Luther, Jean Calvin, straight to the Jesuits.

We are all Roman Catholic. It says it on the school door.
We've cleaned up 'the abuses' with PR machines as
immovable as Croagh Patrick. We will ruin you in this town.
Protestantism allowed a randy king to marry a younger woman,
stands for nothing but leaving your toaster out on the sink.

There was never really a civil war in Ireland.
A few brothers had a fight, down in Cork or West Cork,
or actually I think it was Mayo.
Give it five minutes' class coverage at most.
Actually I don't think you need to teach it at all, there's confession
    that day.

Michelangelo, Petrarch, Raphael, Dürer, now they were all great men.
I could go on. And on. And on. And I will.

2015 is the first year I read a comprehensive list of female
    Renaissance artists, Sofonisba Anguissola was a friend
    of Michelangelo. Bet he copied her.

The Industrial Revolution was a great time, lots of great inventions,
made great by the Agricultural Revolution, lots of food to make
    the men great.

Many women worked in the factories,
I don't know their names.
They only teach about a Spinning Jenny.
And I think this is named after an ass.

In 2007 a doctor tells me I have a brain clot,
I am pregnant, I ask him of the option of a termination.
He tells me that I will change my mind when I am a mother.
'I am a mother,' I say.

I heard three women's names mentioned in my History Class.
Nano Nagle, Constance Markievicz and Mary Robinson.
I try to imagine what they would do.

My first boyfriend punches me seven times on Shop Street
    and we end up in the hospital because he puts his fist
    through the window of a shop my uncle works in
    (bad coincidence). But I am in terror in case anyone
    has recognised me. The shame.

In 1927 women are banned from sitting on juries in Ireland.

History lessons. *In 1935 contraception is banned in Ireland.*

The hospital gives me a card for domestic violence abuse victims.

I am embarrassed at how little they know about me.
And how much I can raise a man's temper.
And my poor ability to mind my men.
I put the card in the bin and withstand another year
for love.

I cannot mind my men. I kept this secret. For now.
I think of Mary Robinson again. I feel a bit of a shit.

It will take a decade before I realise I do not rise temper
    in anyone.
They rise all by themselves. This should be the first lesson.

Mussolini's rise to power was made easy by the colour of their shirts,
    the communists,
the Treaty of Versailles and his March on Rome.

I meet Ariana Reines for the first time in 2015. We drink
    ginger cocktails in a bar in Copenhagen, I promise I will
    use the word cock more in my work.
(cockcockcockcockcock)
    I still cannot come up with a proper name for my own
    cock area. I like the word cunt, but I like to use it angrily
    at those I hate.
(cuntcuntcuntcuntcunt)
    I am blown away by Ms Reines,
    and how the paper won't refuse her ink. I only wish I met
    her sooner.

The 1916 Rising was neither a rebellion nor a revolution;
*   it was a thing apart entirely.*
It was a glorious thing, with god and glory and rising.

And look at us all now.

I ask my class why 1916 makes them happy?
They tell me it's better than being fucking English.
Although a few of them are English, but they like being Irish too.

The men often signed the Solemn League and Covenant in blood.

I correct the use of the word fucking as a race adjective.

I have never taught with an openly gay teacher.

Medieval times meted out some cruel punishments, most of which
*   are still being perfected and used in the world today.*
*   Though most kids will come away thinking knights are cool*
*   and castles had great shooting windows and the past is the*
*   past and the Enlightenment, oh how enlightened it made us all.*
*   Particularly the men, who in turn could choose what to do with*
*   enlightening the women, and all the other races they had to*
*   deal with too.*

Savita Halappanavar dies in October 2012. I cannot stop crying.

2017, My London Bombing Nana is dead and the
Salmon Bedroom Nana is trying hard to remember.

Elaine Feeney is an Irish poet. She has published three collections
with Salmon Poetry, most recently, *Rise* (2017).

7

I DON'T KNOW WHAT I THOUGHT ABORTION WOULD BE LIKE...

CAITLIN MORAN

I cannot understand anti-abortion arguments that centre on the sanctity of life. As a species, we've fairly comprehensively demonstrated that we don't believe in the sanctity of life. The shrugging acceptance of war, famine, epidemic, pain and lifelong, grinding poverty show us that, whatever we tell ourselves, we've made only the most feeble of efforts to *really* treat human life as sacred.

I don't understand, then, why in the midst of all this, pregnant women – women trying to make rational decisions about their futures and, usually, those of their families too – should be subject to more pressure about preserving life than, say, Vladimir Putin, the World Bank or the Catholic Church.

However, what I do believe to be genuinely sacred – and indeed, more useful to the earth as a whole – is trying to ensure that there are as few unbalanced, destructive people as possible. By whatever rationale you use, ending a pregnancy twelve weeks into gestation is incalculably more moral than bringing an unwanted child into this world.

It's those unhappy, unwanted children, who then grew into angry adults, who have caused the great majority of humankind's miseries. They are the ones who make estates feel feral, streets dangerous, relationships violent. If psychoanalysis has, somewhat brutally, laid the responsibility for psychological disorders at parents' doors, the least we can do is to tip our hats to women aware enough not to create those troubled people in the first place.

But, of course, we don't. In the last two years, three bills have been tabled in the Commons seeking to curtail women's access to termination. *The Times* reported that 'unprecedented numbers' of doctors are opting out of terminations, dismayed by the increase in operations.

A great deal of the reason why anti-abortion sentiment is allowed to hold ground in that debate is just that – an ideological, religious or socio-political debate on abortion. It is rarely discussed in terms of personal experience, despite record numbers of women – 189,100 in the UK in 2009 – having them. Every year, an estimated 42 million abortions occur worldwide – 20 million occurring safely, with proper medical supervision, and 22 million occurring unsafely. Across the world, women are doing what they have always done throughout history dealing with a potentially life-altering or life-threatening crisis and then not talking about it afterwards. In case anyone near to them – those people who are not bleeding, and who have not just had an abortion – gets upset.

Women – always loath to talk about the more visceral elements of female reproductive physicality – are too ashamed, or unconfident of their reception, to discuss their terminations, even with friends or partners. This brings about the curious situation in which, while pretty much everyone must have someone dear to them who has had an abortion, the chances of them actually discussing it with their more conservative elders or menfolk are remote.

Consequently, we have a climate where anti-abortionists can discuss abortion as something that 'they' do over 'there', rather than the reality – that it has, in all likelihood, been a calm, rational, well-thought-out act, which has statistically occurred very close to home...

I want to end the pregnancy as quickly as possible, and go straight to see the consultant I had for my last birth. During an awkward five-minute consultation, he has to point out to me that the hospital we are in – St John & St Elizabeth's in St John's Wood – is a Catholic hospital, and I have just, in effect, asked the Pope for an abortion.

Back home, the world's least-fun Google search suggests a consultant in Golders Green, followed by a 'procedure' out in Essex. There are two viable options for the abortion itself – I can either be knocked out and wake up to find it all over but then spend a night in hospital; or I can stay conscious but go home the same day. I am still breastfeeding my youngest – so staying conscious then going home it is.

There is the third option – the 'medical abortion', where you take two pills and then miscarry at home – but, asking around, anyone who's experienced it says, 'It tends to freak you out quite a lot. You just walk around your house bleeding for days. And there's a chance it won't work, and then you'll end up having to have a D & C anyway. Just go in and get it over and done with.'

The clinic we go to is out in Essex, in an area that has that light suburban air of wife-swapping and neat brothels run by bosomy women. I suppose, given its air of offering harbour to humanity's shameful physical needs, this is the right place for an abortion clinic. Inside it reminds me of a Victorian youth hostel – the atmosphere of the 'clients' being up to no good, and the staff watching them quietly from the landing above, purse-mouthed and disapproving.

In the waiting room there are four couples and two women on their own. The younger woman is from Ireland. She arrived here this morning, and apparently – I gather, from what she is whispering to the receptionist – will go back on the ferry tonight.

The older woman looks in her late forties, maybe even early fifties. She cries without making a sound. She has the air of a woman who hasn't told a soul and never will.

The couples are silent, too – all possible conversations have been had before you get here. My husband is red-eyed but solid, just as he was through two births and a miscarriage. He made his definitive statement on all this years ago: 'It seems wildly unfair that, for *us* to reproduce, *you* have to go through all this … shit.'

In the peerlessly unromantic conversation we had, when I phoned him from outside the ultrasound clinic, there wasn't even a debate. He said, 'What do you want to do?' I said, 'No,' and he said, 'Yeah.'

We knew how we both felt – God, we'd lain in bed the week before after spending the day with friends and their newborn, going, 'She's got that Thousand Yard Stare, and he looks half dead. You forget how much *attention* they need, don't you? How you're just … stuck.'

The nurse calls my name and I leave his hand to go to that room. As I walk, I levitate up, up, up into panic attack, and in a telescopic rush, I know – coldly *know* – that I am making a terrible mistake, and that I must keep this baby, no matter what. But I also know panic attacks, and I know their life. Every single other thought you have had has brought you, unfailingly, here, I tell myself. This isn't a last-minute revelation. This is just fear. Tell it to stop.

I don't know what I thought abortion would be like. When I had a D & C after my miscarriage, they knocked me out – weeping – and I woke up – weeping – with it all over.

'Where's the baby?' I kept saying, off my face, as they wheeled me into a room and told me – as gently as possible – to shut up. The only real knowledge I had of that procedure were the after-effects: sore, obviously, and aware of the pregnancy hormones leaving me, hour by hour. Taking away the oestrogen floatiness, and making me feel heavy – my proper gravity – again, like when you stay in a bath reading as the water drains away.

This time, I'm awake for all of it. The whole thing is a bad surprise. I suppose I thought the one thing it would be was 'clinical' – doctors just doing their job coldly and quickly, procedure precise and fast. But as I lie on the bed – the last appointment of the day – the doctors have the air of people who've spent far too long doing unpleasant things in order to rectify the mistakes of others.

You wanted to become a doctor to help people and to feel better at the end of your job, I think, watching them as the nurse takes my hand. But I don't think you do feel better at the end of the day. You look like humans have constantly disappointed you.

The abortion itself is not what I had expected, in that it is both painful and seems fairly crude. The cervix is opened manually with some manner of ratchet. Then a speculum is inserted, and they start to perform the abortion, which appears to be just smashing stuff up with a spoon. It's wincingly violent. Like breaking the yolk of an egg with a chopstick, I think, doing the breathing I learned for labour, which is, of course, a very bad joke.

It's quite painful – like labour, five hours in. The painkiller has been absolutely useless but complaining about pain, given what you are doing, seems inappropriate. Even if you yourself don't believe you should experience pain while having an abortion, there's a distinct atmosphere that the staff here do.

'You're doing fine,' the nurse says, holding my hand very hard. She is kind, but she is also, obviously, already putting her coat on and thinking about getting out the door. She can smell the weekend from here. She is already far away.

The doctor then uses a Vacurette to hoover my womb out, which is pretty much exactly as you'd imagine having the contents of your womb vacuumed out to feel like. In the months after, it makes me repeatedly demur from the purchase of a Black & Decker Dustbuster.

The whole process has taken maybe seven minutes – it is brisk – but the longing for every instrument and hand to retreat from you, and allow you to quietly knit back together and heal, is immense. You want everyone to GET OUT of you. Everyone.

The doctor turns the vacuum off. He then turns it on again and does one last little bit, like when you're doing the front room, finish, and then decide to give the sofa cushions a once-over while you're at it.

Finally, he's done, and I let out an involuntary 'Ahhh!' as his hand withdraws.

'See!' he says, with a firm smile. 'Not too bad! All done!'

Then he looks down into the dish, which holds everything that was inside me. Intrigued by something, he calls his colleague over, from the sluice.

'Look at that!' he says, pointing.

'Hahah – unusual!' the other says.

They both laugh before the dish is carried away and the gloves are peeled off and the cleaning-up starts. The day is now done.

I don't want to ask what it is they have seen. Maybe they could detect he was gay, even at this early stage.

The best thought is: *Perhaps she's hideously deformed, and I would have miscarried her anyway.*

The very worst thought is: *Perhaps something was struggling to stay alive – perhaps he's running out his last piece of luck as I lie here, feeling pale as paper on the outside, and red and black on the inside, like bad meat.* That's the worst bit. The very worst bit. I wish these doctors would shut up.

When they take you into the next room – the 'recovery room' – you lie, wrapped in a towelling robe, on a reclining chair. They give you a magazine and a cold drink. There is a potted palm tree in the corner. It looks like the worst remake of Wham!'s 'Club Tropicana' video ever.

The girl from Ireland leaves after five minutes – she has to catch her bus, to catch her coach, to catch her ferry back home. She walks sore. It's blatantly obvious that she shouldn't have had to come to another country to get her life back on track. I wonder if the judges in Ireland have ever seen a woman as pale as this, counting out fifties onto the reception desk in a country where she doesn't know a soul, and then bleeding all the way from Essex to Holyhead. I wonder if her father approves of the law because he doesn't think it applies to her – and whether he would hate the law if he knew it did, and has brought her here.

The older woman – who was crying silently in the waiting room – is here now, still crying. We all seem to have agreed at some point to pretend that we're not here, so no one catches her eye. We just read the magazines until the forty minutes' 'recovery time' is up and the nurse says, 'You can go.'

And we drive away – with my husband driving dangerously because he's holding my hand very, very tight – I say, 'I'm going to get the contraceptive version of Trident fitted, I think,' and he says, 'Yeah,' and holds my hand even tighter. And that is the end of the day.

Give the subject matter, it seems odd to say that this is the happy ending – but it is.

All accounts of abortion that I have seen always had, as dolorous coda, how the procedure left a mark. However female-sympathetic the publication, there is a need to mention how the anniversary of the abortion is always remembered with sorrow – the baby's due date marked with a sudden flood of tears.

The narrative is that while a woman may tell herself, rationally, that she couldn't have that baby, there will be a part of her that does not believe this – which carries on silently marking the baby that should have come. Women's bodies do not give up their babies so easily, and so silently, is the message. The heart will always remember.

This is what I expect. But this is not how it is. Indeed, it's the opposite. I keep waiting for my prescribed grief and guilt to come – I am braced, chest out, ready – but it never arrives. I don't cry when I see baby clothes. Friends announcing pregnancies don't make me jealous or quietly blue. I do not have to remind myself that sometimes you must do the 'wrong' thing for the 'right' reason.

In fact, it's the opposite. Every time I sleep through the night, I am thankful for the choice I have made. When the youngest graduates out of nappies, I'm relieved there isn't a third one following behind. When friends come round with their new babies, I am hugely, hugely grateful that I had the option not to do this again – and that that option didn't involve me lying on a friend's kitchen table after the kids had gone to sleep, praying I wouldn't get an infection or haemorrhage to death before I got home.

I talk to other friends about this after a few drinks, and they agree.

'I walk past playgrounds thinking, *If I'd gone through with the pregnancy, I'd still be sitting on that bench, fat, depressed, knackered, and just waiting for my life to start again*,' Lizzie says.

Rachel is, as always, brisker. 'It's one of the top four best things I ever did – after marrying my husband, having my son and getting a fixed quote on the loft conversion.'

I suppose what I'd been given to believe is that my body – or my subconscious – would be *angry* with me for not having the baby. And that, additionally, their opinion on the matter would, in some way, be superior – more 'natural', more moral – to the rational decision my conscious mind had made. That women were made to have babies, and that each one that is not brought to fruition must be accounted and mourned and repented for, and would remain unforgiven forever.

But all I could see – and all I can see now, years later – is history made of millions of women trying to undo the mistake that could undo them, and then just carrying on, quiet, thankful and silent about the whole thing. What I see is that it can be an action with only good consequence.

Caitlin Moran is an award-winning journalist, author and screenwriter. She is a columnist with *The Times*. Her books include *How to Be a Woman* (2011), *Moranthology* (2012), *How to Build a Girl* (2014) and *Moranifesto* (2016).

8

INFINITE FOR NOW
SINÉAD GLEESON

Day 1

You can spell blood with your hands, he says, curling his index
fingers and thumbs into 'b' and 'd'. Wrists bent back, ring finger
forming a boxy 'o'. This presents an excuse to stare at his arms,
the strong cables of his veins. The grass beneath them is cool,
and the fire hisses. The leaves give out a damp tang, turning
the smoke green. Breath quickens and she knows this feeling,
the one everyone chases. This firstness. The dilated pupil, the
curved mouth hint, the victory. Orion is above them, his belt
hazy behind clouds, and she stares at Betelgeuse, glinting in the
blackness. His shoulder moves, and she readies herself for the
lean in. A tentative brush, then parted lips and the full warmth
of his mouth. *Yes!* she thinks, with a definite exclamation mark.
Someone cheers from the bodies huddled on the other side of
the fire. Up there, Bellatrix, Epsilon and Delta peer down at this
new thing. The bones of it barely knitted together.

Day 3

She isn't beautiful, she knows this. People say she is funny, but
that's not the same. Her brothers have a band and when she

watches them play, their long hair grazing tremolo arms, she thinks she could be a singer. And she'll write songs about how beauty isn't important, how it's No. Big. Deal. But he's beautiful. Too beautiful, that's the problem. There is no level of girl he couldn't get, no woman he couldn't make stare at him. He has never been turned down, or told no. But from the redness of that kiss, and all those stars, he came back again. To her.

Day 5

Text messages pile up into a satisfying amount, enough to call a history. A heap of emojis, the occasional misspelling, two dots, not three in every ellipsis. She likes to imagine that she is the missing dot.

Day 8

A darkened cinema with velvet curtains. Something subtitled, French. Lip-locked and panting, a crescent of blood bruises on her neck.

'Lovebites? Are they still a thing?' asks her father.

'Be careful,' says her mother, who talks for ten minutes without a breath about how a girl can ruin her life. How the horizon can vanish, and take all the blue with it.

Day 10

Guitar strumming. The heavy mahogany pressing against her thigh, and she remembers his hardness by the fire. Mind wanders, followed by hands. *I will not write a song about him. I will NOT write a song about him.* Fingers in jeans, and then ache, and bliss.

She writes a song about him.

Day 12

Her parents depart for a cruise. For years there was never any money for holidays, but now they're off down the Danube. She imagines her father throwing back Pilsner, her mother ordering one glass of Riesling over the whole week. Friday, and her brothers depart in the diesel rumble of the band van, sweating and swilling cans on the drive to Galway. The sun tilts, and in the quiet she shaves her legs, prepares her face, siphons a replaceable amount of gin from a blue bottle.

At night it never gets hot here, even in summer months. There are no chirping crickets, no hiss of sprinklers, nothing that could be mistaken for balmy. It's spring, but feels like summer. They lie in her single bed, bodies asking questions of each other. He stretches up to open a window, a pale pillar in the dim light. His veins bulge, electricity filling up the room.

'Let's pretend we're somewhere else.'

'Eh, like where?'

'New York.'

'What's wrong with London?'

'Too near. Same shite weather.'

'OK... so... New York?'

'Look, just close your eyes. Now. Close them and listen.'

They tune themselves to the noise of the city, which responds and rises up. Horns beeping, girls shrieking. The recalibration was instant and surprising.

'Music, or no music?'

He gestures towards the spines of CDs stacked to cover the black mould on the wall. She eyes the curve of his cigarette ash, bending towards the floor, just as he flicks it into a glass; a marionette movement.

'Music. Yay or nay?'

She can't decide if a soundtrack is appropriate or not. If – after Woody Allen and Scorsese, and dozens of films about gangsters and broads, and cars bigger than boats and streets like crossword puzzles – it's even possible to put that city into music. And New York and its vastness make her feel afraid, even though she is here, in an old terraced house in Dublin. The light, or the slightly menacing shape of his shoulders, or what's happening between them... something makes the sense of abandon disappear. *Cop on*, she thinks, *don't spoil this.*

'No music,' she says.

And then a beat, before something comes to her and she wants that feeling back, the one she had upon opening the door and finding him standing there.

'Wait. *Rhapsody in Blue.*'

He smiles, impressed, but chooses to counter-attack.

'C'mon! The fucking Ramones, surely!'

But neither moves. He lies back, pressing his body to hers, still sweat-slicked, his elbow jutting like a jetty into the sea of her skin.

'I'm a bad sleeper.'

She had noticed the under-eye grey, the only distracting thing about his face. Later, she wakes, dead-armed from curling into him, and sees him scrolling and scrolling, the blue light interrupting the dark.

Day 13

The weekend moves too quickly. Tomorrow, her brothers will be back, although they'd cover for her. Tonight, they go for a drink, him downing Guinness, her on the pale ale, and end up crashing someone's party, jumping around to nostalgic tunes for people over forty. The walk home takes an hour. They stop to lean against walls and devour each other.

Day 14

He has to leave early, and departs after three failed attempts to get out the door. Bells peal from the church at the end of the street, and this morning she doesn't mind them lobbing a bomb into her weekend hangover. Her father complains that the new apartments beside them block the light, but she likes their closeness. People moving behind the glass, kids playing in the stairwell. You're never alone in a city. For weeks, she watched a couple preparing a nursery on the second floor. Painting walls in neutral yellow, building a cot, the woman hanging coloured bunting around the room. Her belly swelling with newness. She sought them out most nights as they curled up on the couch, laughing at TV. Their happiness a finish line, something she craved. And then it was quiet. No lights for days. The man eventually returned and took the cot apart. A Latvian family lives there now. They leave the windows open all year round.

Day 18
A card arrives in the post. An actual card in an envelope. Like something from the 1980s. It says 'hook, line and sinker'. She doesn't know if this is a good or bad thing.

Day 23
In the forest below the hill, he chases her through the trees. They laugh, like people in films who are in love. 'I'm not a deer, you know!' She slows to let him catch her. The green cools their heat, until his hands are on her, his breath on her neck, and she focuses on the spruce trees, his shudders.

Day 29
New York is on her mind. She imagines them in the Lower East Side, or sipping beer on a stoop in Brooklyn. That bridge over the Hudson that movie gangsters have meetings under. Then the hops from Guinness, its burnt cream, drifts out over the Liffey

and Dublin, nudging away the skyscrapers, reminding her of all that this city is and has been. This place that she loves and hates.

Day 34

They climb the hill again, sinking into the gloom of the forest floor. Their dedication is athletic. Triathlon level, even. After, they squint against the too-bright city; the yellow lights douse whatever stars might be up there. She passes her phone to him, app open.

'What?' His smile lopsided.

'Here. Point it upwards.'

'We said to put phones away. What?'

'Watch.'

She holds the phone aloft and Hercules and Pegasus charge on to the ceiling. He takes it, tilts and rolls until stars and planets appear. Andromeda, Mercury at the tail of Pisces' fish, the Moon below Aries. Constellations swoop by, joined up by lines on the screen. Digital dots doubling for the ones the city night sky has hidden. He drops the phone and there are kisses. Hundreds of them, hot as the hydrogen burning in every dusted star. An ambulance streaks by, each oscillating wail rises and dips, as if the sound itself is a country road. He traces crescents on her back. Not celestial bodies, but infinite for now.

Day 35

They talk of getting the bus to Sligo for a weekend. Swimming and a seaweed bath; he wants her to try surfing. Then a climb to the top of Knocknarea, to visit Queen Maeve's tomb. Survey the limestone slant of Benbulbin and the wide Atlantic. Next stop across the ocean: New York. There are always more stars in the countryside.

Day 36

She types and deletes the message eight times.

Wanna go to Brooklyn again, or take a spin around the stars?
Text sent.
Delivered.

Day 37

It's seventeen hours since the last text. The WhatsApp messages say delivered and read. Pacing the house, she retreads the stairs, wondering if she was too much, or not enough. Girls are always too something. Phone in hand, palms sweating the screen, willing something to appear. She turns off all notifications except messaging apps, cursing each stupid 'like' that causes it to buzz.

Day 38

The nights are full of sweat, islanded in her own saltwater. Dreams of people with no eyes, the forest, of specimen jars – full of what, she doesn't know – in colourless suspension.

Day 39

Her mother starts with the questions. A machine-gun approach, of not listening, of raising the tone a little – a plane taking off – with each enquiry.

'I don't know, Ma.
'Leave it.
Please?'

Day 40

Calculations.

Days since last text.
Times they've been together.
Hours without him, without that.

Calendars.
Communication.
Constellations.
Betelgeuse blinking at her up on that hill. The moon taking its white hulk off behind the clouds, offering them the darkness.

Day 41

Easter approaches. All Jesus and death and resurrection. And pink lakes of cherry blossoms pooled under trees, and hailstones, even though May is almost on top of them. And sans serif words blinking in a plastic window.

Day 43
Search.
    Click.
    Confirm.
    Click.
    Clear cache.

Day 44

Crying brings on constant headaches, stinging eyes. She is sick of tears, mortified by her own wailing.

'It happens to everyone, you know.'

In the doorway, her mother's pose is firmly one of passing by, not contemplated entry. This is fine. She doesn't want her to come in. And then a sudden longing for her mother's arms around her is a surprise.

'Look, love. You think your father and I weren't young once? Oh, I turned many heads, I can tell you.'

She watches her mother's reverie trick of folding her arms, head tilted to the past.

'It wasn't—'

She presses her eyes into the pillow, which is salted and snot-streaked.

'He just—'

'I know love, I know. You'll get over it. You have to kiss a lot of fr—'

'DON'T,' she mutters from the depths of the bed.

Day 46

Today, she burns sage, burns the card, burns skin where the first bite was. Where purple went yellow, now red and fizzing. She picks at it in the bath.

Day 47

I'm Maeve. Queen fucking Maeve, she says to herself. *Not buried upright under stones, but still ready for battle. I've got my swords; I'll take you all on.*

Queen, queen, queen, she whispers.

Day 48

She should never have told him, but it was in that post-physical, post-sweat, post-grapple moment. Those dizzy, content seconds where there is the same energy as after a fight. The compulsion to overshare, to reveal, to confess. The overwhelming urge to give another person a secret morsel of yourself that says, 'We're fine, I trust you, and this is how much.' Maybe she should have settled for asking: 'What are you thinking?' But on that night, of Hercules and Andromeda, it slipped into the air like an eel, curling around their joined bodies.

I'm late.

This makes her think of meetings, or missed buses or her body failing to get over a finish line like a runner with jellied legs.

Day 50

Her stomach acclimatises to the height as the plane sweeps out over the bay. Past the candy stripes of Poolbeg Towers, and below, a ferry making a white furrow of the sea. Far from the slab of her single bed, far from handbag naggins and from the arrow of his spine. It hurts to think of his body, the flesh and bones of him. The wing tilts, disappearing the sea. *We are beginning our descent into London Gatwick.*

Day 52

In two days, she's back home. Waking to her brother strumming a guitar at the end of her bed, softly singing a song she loves. One they used to sing as kids. Her throat has little air, not enough for words or a chorus. His fingers move along the frets and he offers a smile, which she tries to answer. The radio drifts up from the kitchen, post drops through the letterbox. Someone is going all out with a Kango hammer outside. *Today*, she thinks. *Today.*

Day 65

The days are getting longer, heating up. Summer arrives full of swagger and possibility: barbecues and cans in the park, festivals and walking home from parties at dawn. There will be places to avoid, but it will be OK.

Day 90

Turns on phone.

Text ping.

Alright? Smiley face.

Ninety days since Betelgeuse on the hill. Not months or a year, but it feels like it. She walks the hill most weekends, in daylight, among the pines and the moss. The blackbirds in the forest are silent by summer. A logging truck wheezes past, teasing the roadside ferns, and she watches the trunks receding down the track. Concentric rings telling a story.

I have a story.

This year will be just one more circle. There will be another when her mother is no longer here, and one for her father, her brothers.

She will forget the circles of Os he made with his hands.

But now, yes, she can spell blood with her whole body now.

Day 4,591

His New York apartment looks expensive. His children are gorgeous, rust-haired. This doesn't look like a curated version of happiness. Clicking through his photos, annoyed by her voyeurism. He is happy. There are soft-filtered images of him holding hands with a tall, blonde woman: on a beach, at Machu Picchu, at dinner parties, their apartment looking out over the gleam of New York, the Chrysler Building just blocks away. Her view is of the sea, and the small island in the bay that she can finally swim to, after years of practice. Cormorants and kittiwakes nest on the cliff above, and at night she switches off the radio and calls the dog. Walking into the dark, breathing in salt and the sharp Atlantic spray, waiting to see where Orion is.

Sinéad Gleeson is a Dublin-based writer who has just completed her first book, a collection of essays.

9

WE WILL WIN BECAUSE WE HAVE TRUTH AND RIGHT ON OUR SIDE

COLM O'GORMAN

As I write this, we do not yet have a date or wording for the referendum on the Eighth Amendment, nor any clear sense of what sort of legal and medical framework will replace it. In fact, we only have a verbal commitment from the Taoiseach that there will be a referendum. Much is yet unknown, and there is a lot of work yet to be done.

But one thing is already certain; the campaign to repeal the Eighth Amendment has already had enormous and important impact. That the 2016 Programme for Government contained an express commitment to reviewing the Eighth Amendment was a massive achievement. That a Citizens' Assembly was indeed created in the same year without endless foot-dragging, and that it overwhelmingly voted for the complete erasure of the Eighth Amendment from the Constitution as well as an expansive legal and medical framework for abortion access, has been extraordinary. This campaign has shown what can be achieved through determined, steadfast and collective effort by civil society, by ordinary individuals who do not hold high office but are relentless in holding their elected representatives to account. This the ideal on which Amnesty International was founded; that every voice counts, and counts most when raised together. The coordinated and cooperative approach by civil society organisations – playing to individual strengths in evidence gathering, advocacy and mobilisation, and sharing ideas and resources – has been tremendous, and it has been an honour for Amnesty International Ireland, of which I am executive director, to be part of it over the past three years.

What has also been remarkable about this campaign is the global solidarity it has captured, both from within the existing women's rights movement but also through the emergence of specific campaign groups like the London-Irish Abortion Rights Campaign. Ireland's abortion laws are of concern to people all across the world. Indeed, within Amnesty International, sections in every continent took action on our 2015–16 global campaign on Ireland's abortion laws, collecting 276,861 signatures calling for the repeal of the Eighth Amendment. Important, too, is global solidarity between campaigners in Ireland and those working for sexual and reproductive rights elsewhere. A recent example was the support for Polish NGOs' black protest, the pro-choice protests in Poland where demonstrators wore black, which was organised to stem the proposed erosion of abortion access there. Similarly, Amnesty International members and supporters here in Ireland have strongly supported our campaigns for expanded access to abortion in Latin America, as well as other sexual and reproductive rights issues in many other regions.

In its work, Amnesty International sees first-hand how domestic women's rights movements are fighting the same battle across the world. The global backlash against women's human rights, particularly those related to women's bodily integrity

Strike4Repeal encouraged women and others across Ireland to strike on
8 March, International Women's Day, 2017. The strike generated
conversation and publicity, and was a definite success, with demonstrations
taking place around the country. Strike4Repeal illustrated the power of
disobedience and direct action as a tactic in the movement.

In July 2016, the artist Maser painted a mural on the Project Arts Centre in Temple Bar as part of a HunReal Issues campaign to repeal the Eighth Amendment. Although broadly supported, the mural created massive public debate when anti-choice complainants attempted to have it removed using planning laws. Maser painted over the mural, and its disappearance ended up potentially being more powerful than its initial appearance, as the image became amplified and replicated around the city.

Hannah Hogan's striking denim jacket designs featured in a Repeal-related exhibition at the Copperhouse Gallery in Dublin. This design is based on an illustration by Adam Hurley.

One of numerous twists on Maser's mural, were these leggings by Isleen Design, a collaboration with the HunReal Issues and Maser.

Out of the Shadows was an artistic awareness-raising project led by Will St Leger and supported by the Abortion Rights Campaign and Amnesty International Ireland, which visited six counties in six days, displaying the 'shadows' of people travelling from Ireland for abortions.

Guts, an independent magazine of confessional writing, published an issue themed 'Fight Back' in 2017, dedicated to women fighting back on all issues affecting their lives. The all-female contributor line-up included illustrators such as Aoife Dooley, Laura Callaghan, Fuchsia Macaree and more.

An image created by Jill & Gill in collaboration with the Repeal Project, and in support of repealing the Eighth Amendment. The image was inspired by Brendan Courtney, who posted a photograph of himself on Instagram with his hands making a figure '8'.

and reproductive and sexual freedoms, can be starkly seen in US President Trump's imposition of the 'global gag rule'. This blocks US federal funding for non-governmental organisations that provide abortion counselling or referrals, advocate to decriminalise abortion or expand abortion services anywhere in the world, and will have a dangerous impact on the sexual and reproductive rights, health and life of women and girls across the world, particularly those who are most at risk of human rights abuses.

The move against women's rights is evidenced in laws that seek to restrict access to reproductive health services, including abortion and family planning in states across the USA and around the world. As I write, in Brazil the National Congress is seeking to introduce laws that would impose a full ban on abortion, including in cases where pregnancy results from rape or involves risk to the mother's life. In addition, Congress is considering proposals that will remove all information on sexual and reproductive health from the syllabus of primary and secondary schools. Across the world we are witnessing an unprecedented attack on women's rights.

This backlash is played out on the floors of the United Nations too. One striking example was the 2015 Human Rights Council resolution on 'protection of the family' proposed by Egypt and other like-minded states. While seeming innocuous, it underhandedly sought to divert the Council from its mandated focus on the rights of individuals towards protecting the purported rights of a social institution, namely, 'the family'. It would have subordinated the human rights of individual members of 'the family', especially women and girls, to the protection of the institution, thereby turning a blind eye to laws, policies and practices that violate or lead to the violation of women's and girls' rights within families. Thankfully, it was voted down.

While discrimination against women is evident in almost all areas of life, it is in the area of sexual and reproductive health that it reaches shocking levels. It is the regulation of women's sexuality and reproduction that most clearly reveals harmful gender stereotypes and bias.

This is why success in overturning the Eighth Amendment will be of far greater magnitude and resonance than its impact in Ireland. It will strike a blow for women's and girls' rights everywhere.

This potential global significance is also why we will see a continued and concerted effort to derail, distract and confuse the abortion debate in Ireland. Some anti-choice groups will be obvious in their mendacity: unfounded assertions that abortions cause breast cancer, child abuse, mental ill health and so on. Some will launch personalised attacks on the professional and personal integrity of campaigners. This can indeed do damage, so we must support each other in weathering that. (It is perhaps no surprise that politicians and the media shy away from considered and objective analysis of the issue when it may result in a deluge of abuse or complaints.)

Others will be more insidious and cunning. What are profoundly ideological positions will be masked as concern for women, for people with disabilities, for Irish society. We already see accusations that the Repeal campaign targets children with disabilities like Down Syndrome, that campaigners are anti-Catholic, that we don't care about women harmed by their abortion decisions. Anti-choice groups will continue to proclaim that women do not have a human right to access safe and legal abortion and that Amnesty International is making up human rights law to suit its agenda. They will keep up their false claim that right-to-life protections set forth in international and regional human rights treaties are accorded before birth, thereby prohibiting states from allowing abortions; that the Convention on the Rights of the Child bestows foetal rights. They will continue to solicit foreign funding for their campaigning (against human rights, I should add), and rail against the Repeal campaign and our funders when we do. We can expect to see more red herrings like the 'babies left alone to die in corners' in the UK, or statements that women are being coerced to have abortions by medical professionals, without any evidence to support these claims. In all the noise and heat they try to generate, we will keep reminding the public that these groups are not telling the truth, and that they represent a tiny minority of the population.

Anti-choice groups will want to make this public and political conversation on abortion about numbers – claims of 12,000, 100,000, 8 million lives saved or ended – as they will think this will change hearts and minds. Repeal supporters will make it clear that this is not a zero-sum game; that abortion bans do not substantially reduce abortions; that where the law does actually serve its end and denies a women or girl an abortion, it is effectively forcing her to remain pregnant, depriving her of dignity and autonomy. We will recognise that there is a spectrum of personal positions on abortion. We will remind people that, whatever they may feel about the morality of terminating a pregnancy, the incontestable fact remains that restrictive abortion laws and other measures serve only to make the procedure less accessible and less safe. We will keep explaining that abortion restrictions impact less on the privileged; they most harm those who already experience discrimination and disadvantage – including economic hardship, uncertain migration status making it difficult to travel – and young women. While many appear happy to overlook or ignore the impact Ireland's abortion ban has on the health and well-being of women and girls, it will continue to be at the heart of all our work on this issue.

We will insist that it is the broader story of women's equality, dignity and human rights that deserves public and political attention. If we tell this story, I am confident that people in Ireland will understand this. This was demonstrated not only in the two-thirds vote of the Citizens' Assembly for access to abortion on request in early pregnancy that so floored the media and politicians, but in the individual Assembly members' comments in the report published in June. People in Ireland can see the terrible harm and suffering Ireland's abortion laws cause. What they want are solutions, and we will help shape and frame those.

We will win, because we have truth and right on our side. We will succeed with evidence and facts, and by appealing to the common sense, good judgement and, above all, compassion and kindness of people in Ireland; by responding to the venom and vitriol with cool heads, calm logic, quiet determination and a modicum of humour where the efforts are actually laughable.

However, to win decisively, we critically need the media and politicians in Ireland to be more incisive and discerning in the attention, space and time given to anti-choice campaigners. There are agendas at work that are about far more than foetal life, and it is to their advantage if abortion is cast as a complicated, controversial and divisive issue. If abortion was once so in Ireland, it is no longer. Polling that we and others have conducted have borne this out. There is a remarkable level of consensus among people in Ireland that our abortion legislation is abusive, and must be brought into line with international human rights standards. The Irish public overwhelmingly shares our demand for change. How the broadcast media's interpretation of equal time given to both sides of a referendum argument is enforced on those who advocate for and those who campaign against a woman's right to access abortion is grotesquely disproportionate to the way society views this issue. The independent poll RED C conducted on behalf of Amnesty International Ireland in 2016 found that only 5 per cent of people in Ireland personally object to abortion in all circumstances; and even, at that, half of that 5 per cent say they would still vote to repeal the Eighth Amendment. It is highly irrational to devote so much airtime and column inches to groups that represent the views of just 2.5 per cent of the population.

As someone working in a human rights organisation and who is passionate about human rights, it has been heartening to see the role that the international human rights framework is playing in this campaign. Civil society organisations are articulating cogent human-rights-based arguments for change, and making full use of the UN's human rights mechanisms. Just this year, Irish NGOs have twice gone to Geneva to make sure that abortion is on the radar of two UN treaty bodies – the Committee on the Elimination of Discrimination Against Women and the Committee Against Torture – in their periodic reviews of Ireland's human rights record.

This is precisely how the human rights framework should be used. It is not the preserve of lawyers and academics. Human rights are basic rights and freedoms to which all people are entitled regardless of nationality, sex, national or ethnic origin, 'race', religion, language or other status. They are the cornerstone of the rule of law and an essential instrument with which states are to ensure that all people are able to live in dignity and freedom. We do not have to sit passively by and hope our governments bestow us our rights. We can and must claim them. We surely also have a moral responsibility to demand rights for those less able to do so for themselves.

It is precisely because of the power of human rights that those opposed to change seek to undermine their very foundation. They wilfully pretend that the UN's human rights treaty bodies (comprised of independent experts elected by states, including Ireland, and created by states to be the guardians of the treaties) are self-appointed quangos. They purposefully confuse these bodies with the UN Human Rights Council (comprised of state representatives, including states with poor human rights records like Saudi Arabia). They deny the legitimacy of the UN's human rights mechanisms' interpretation of the treaties (that is their job, as mandated by states like Ireland). They carefully avoid suggesting that they simply disagree with international human rights standards that do not suit them, and instead attack how that law has evolved since the treaties were drafted. They will try to assert that the treaties, as written decades ago, must be read literally and rigidly.

All the while, we will keep repeating the truth. Access to abortion is a human rights issue, and as long as the Eighth Amendment remains in the Irish Constitution and the laws that flow from it remain in place, Ireland will be in breach of the legal obligations it voluntarily signed up to when it ratified the human rights treaties.

There is also a regrettable reluctance on the part of the Irish government to fully back the legal authority of these mechanisms. The former Taoiseach, Enda Kenny, was reported in the media as responding to the UN Committee Against Torture's questioning Ireland on abortion by saying that this committee is not a court and therefore its views are not legally binding. In ratifying these treaties, the Irish state voluntarily assumed internationally legally binding obligations and duties to respect, to protect and to fulfil human rights, and undertake to ensure that our domestic laws are compatible with the treaty obligations and duties. In ratifying these treaties, Ireland has solemnly undertaken to comply in good faith with their obligations. Ireland has helped create and then elect the treaty bodies to determine the nature of these obligations. It is disingenuous to create this architecture and then deny its authority. So we must continue to defend the legitimacy of international human rights standards.

The international human rights framework can and does help us shape the government's agendas and priorities. For instance, the UN Human Rights Committee's June 2016 decision in *Mellet v. Ireland*, finding Ireland had violated the International Covenant on Civil and Political Rights, was indeed a game changer. The decision laid bare the trauma and anguish that Ireland's abortion laws inflicted on the woman who took the case, Amanda Mellet, thereby shedding light on the stories of countless others who have had to travel abroad to find the healthcare they needed. The government could not and did not deny that what had happened to Ms Mellet amounted to cruel, inhuman or degrading treatment, or that her rights to privacy and equality had also been violated.

In June 2017, in *Whelan v. Ireland*, that same committee not only found the same violations, but additionally determined that Ireland's abortion law amounts to gender discrimination because it denies women access to a medical service only women need. Taking these cases to the UN were acts of tremendous courage. It should not be necessary for women to have to do this, but it worked.

The UN Committee Against Torture's concluding observations on Ireland's first periodic report in 2011 made the government finally pay attention to the human rights abuses carried out in the Magdalene Laundries. Of course the government's response to that has been deeply unsatisfactory, but the UN's treaty bodies have seen that and have relentlessly continued to hold the State to account.

The international human rights framework can guide the legislation and medical provision to replace the Eighth Amendment we are seeking – i.e., the human rights principles of equality and non-discrimination, and women's rights to physical integrity, health, privacy and autonomous decision-making on matters related to sexuality and reproduction. It can also help navigate different sets of values and rights. The framework was created to ensure that all individuals' rights were protected by the State in spite of tensions arising from differences over political or religious ideologies, and social or moral norms. Of course, freedom of conscience, religion or belief are important and must be respected, as they do find expression in international human rights treaties, but they cannot be allowed by the State to erode or violate the rights of women and girls. This applies equally to medical providers refusing to provide abortions for reasons of conscience. In fact, Amnesty International's polling on abortion found that attitudes around abortion in Ireland varied little depending on whether or not people are religious. It found that 82 per cent of people who consider themselves religious do not want their religious views imposed on others. Also, of course, states may protect foetal interests, but as a part of the healthcare provided to pregnant women, not as rights to be balanced against the human rights of a pregnant woman or girl. The states themselves determined that international human rights law applies to people after they have been born.

As I said, it will be important that the campaign to repeal the Eighth Amendment identifies and counters the tactics adopted by some of those opposed to reform. However, we must avoid becoming preoccupied by them. Instead we must focus on continuing our honest, objective and evidence-based public education and campaigning. Those who work to oppose women's reproductive rights cannot block out the truth or prevent the kind of progress supported by the majority of people.

We must focus on what we have learned from flawed legislative approaches in other jurisdictions and in Ireland. Irish people can see the obstacle course the Protection of Life During Pregnancy Act is. It is unworkable. It is clear that restrictive abortion laws, which provide only for narrow, minimum grounds, can never realise the human rights of women and girls. People understand that when it comes to decisions about women's bodies, health and lives, it is time for women to make those decisions. In recent decades people in Ireland have had cause to examine very dark aspects of Irish history. We have had to face difficult truths about how we treated women and girls in our republic. We have learned lessons, and now we must apply them.

To properly understand the Eighth Amendment, it and Ireland's abortion laws must be viewed in the context of the historical suppression and control of women's sexuality and reproduction. The Eighth Amendment was part of a broader social and political context in which the State and religious institutions have subjected women and girls to strict, punitive social controls around their sexuality and reproduction. Stereotypes about women's roles in society and their sexual conduct were also violently enforced by the State and religious institutions through the Magdalene Laundries and Mother and Baby Homes. The last Magdalene Laundry closed in 1996, the same year that the last Mother and Baby Home also closed its doors.

That time is past, but its legacy lingers. We must move on. We need to be truly feel free to look at abortion by today's standards, which is in terms of women's and girls' human rights. We need to trust women to make the decisions about their bodies, health and lives.

Colm O'Gorman is the executive director of
Amnesty International Ireland.

10

WE FACE THIS LAND
SARAH MARIA GRIFFIN

Centuries ago,
Women accused of witchcraft faced, amongst other ordeals,
Trial by water

Tied to a chair or run under a boat
If she survives the drowning and floats
She's a witch. If she dies, she's a woman

We are not witches but if the church and state insists
Then let us be the descendants of all the witches they could
  not drown
This heirloom of trauma, this curse

This agony of water in order to hold agency over our bodies
Not all of us have survived, the waves do not part
There are no miracles here

When the stethoscope is a crucifix on your belly
How do you have any choice but the water
And fair medical treatment on another

A body is a body is a body is a body is a body is a body is a body
Not a house. Not a city. Not a vessel, not a country
The laws of the church have no place on your flesh

A veterinarian will abort a calf if a cow is falling ill. How is it
    that livestock is
worth more to this land than us?

Eleven women every day leave Ireland seeking an
abortion abroad.

We ask for the land over the water. Home over trial. Choice
    over none.
For our foremothers, ourselves, the generations yet to come
Witches or women – these are our bodies which shall not be
    given up

Sarah Maria Griffin is a poet and novelist.

11

WE MARCHED AND WE WILL MARCH AGAIN

LOUISE O'NEILL

It is Saturday, 24 September 2016. My alarm goes off at 5.45 a.m. It is dark outside, but I can hear the rain beating against my window and all I want to do is pull the duvet over my head and go back to sleep. But I don't. I don't because today is important. I leave the house at 7 a.m., my father warning me of flooded roads and urging me to 'drive slowly'. He doesn't like it when I drive in this kind of weather, but he doesn't tell me to stay at home either. He knows that today is important too.

On the train to Dublin, I try and nap, but I can't stop scrolling through my Twitter feed. There are messages of support from all over the world, similar protests being planned in London, Montreal, Paris, Berlin, New York. I can feel my excitement build as I see the photos of other people making their journey to Dublin, of their refusal to be deterred by the inclement weather. *We are walking in the rain*, my friend Dave tweets, *to support thousands of women who have to face an ocean*. As I disembark, an elderly woman grabs my hand. She has seen my sweater, she tells me. 'Thank you,' she says. '*Thank you*.' She walks away before I can reply and I am left wondering about her and the countless other women of her generation who smile sadly when they see the sweatshirts 'the young people' are wearing these days, the word *Repeal* picked out in white letters on black cotton. What stories do these women have? What secrets have they kept? And for how long?

I battle my way through the crowds at the Garden of Remembrance. The number of people here seems almost incomprehensible. Tens of thousands of people, men and women, young and old, marching together because we believe in empathy and kindness. We think that women should have the basic human right to bodily autonomy. We trust women.

The sense of solidarity is incredible. There are whispers that celebrities are marching, that Cillian Murphy and Hozier are standing with us. I see people I know and we hug one another. We say how glad we are to be here, to be a part of this movement. There is a ripple of something powerful moving through the crowd, as if our footsteps are rupturing the earth beneath us, shattering an archaic status quo. It feels as if something is shifting, like real change is finally imminent. The atmosphere is hopeful, buoyant almost. I had joked that I didn't care about the rain, that my righteous anger would keep me warm, but in the end it was a sense of overwhelming love that infused me. Love for my gals who were walking beside me, for my friend Louise who marched despite being forty weeks pregnant, for the people passing by who clapped and cheered us on, for the organisers who worked tirelessly and thanklessly to ensure the event would go ahead. There are so many Repeal sweatshirts, and each time I see one, I feel so proud of Anna Cosgrave for what she has created. Just one person and an idea. Sometimes that's all it takes, in the end.

But no matter how joyous the march is, I cannot help but think of the women who travelled before us, fled these shores in order to get the help they needed. Their ghosts walk with us, hungry, alone, scared, their mouths sewn shut by a Church and a State that tried to silence them with shame. I mouth the words of 'We Face This Land', the poem by Sarah Griffin.

> 'A body is a body is a body is a body is a body is a body
>   is a body
> Not a house. Not a city. Not a vessel, not a country.
> The laws of the church have no place on your flesh.

> A veterinarian will abort a calf if a cow is falling ill.
>   How is it that livestock is
> worth more to this land than us?...

> We ask for the land over the water. Home over trial.
>   Choice over none.
> For our foremothers, ourselves, the generations yet
>   to come.
> Witches or women – these are our bodies which shall
>   not be given up.'

We will not be silenced any more. We will not be shamed. For these are our bodies, our decisions. Our lives.

Sometimes I wonder what I would have done if I had lived in a different time from now. Would I have raged against racism in 1940s Mississippi? Would I have refused to be swept along in a wave of anti-Semitic fever if I had lived in Nazi Germany? Would I have fought for women's suffrage in the early twentieth century despite the social and personal consequences? Would I have travelled to Belfast on the Contraception Train in 1971? Would I have been brave, I ask myself? Or would I have stayed silent for the sake of an easy life? It's impossible to know, of course, but as

I was sitting on the train home to Cork that evening, shivering in my wet clothes, I felt a sense of peace. I was glad I had been there and that when it came to my chance to stand up for what it is right, I had done so. I was glad that when, in years to come, people shake their heads in horror at the barbarism of forcing women to travel abroad to avail themselves of often life-saving medical treatment, I will be able to say that I did my bit. I will be able to say that I was on the right side of history, that I stood up and fought for equality.

And I wasn't alone. There were thousands of us. We marched for the pregnant housewife denied cancer treatment for fear of harming her unborn child. For the fourteen-year-old girl who was raped by a neighbour and prevented from travelling for an abortion by the Attorney General. For Savita [Halappanavar] who died crying out for a termination and who was told this is 'a Catholic country'. For a woman kept artificially alive to prolong the heartbeat of the foetus in her womb. For the woman who sought asylum in Ireland and who found she was trapped here in a very different way, her body becoming a prison she couldn't escape from. And we marched for the ten to twelve women a day who continue to travel for basic healthcare, the women we have forced into exile, the women we have made criminals of and told to keep their secrets for fear of recrimination and judgement.

We marched. And we will march again.

We will keep marching until our voices are heard.

Louise O'Neill is an award-winning novelist and author of *Only Ever Yours*, *Asking For It*, *Almost Love* and *The Surface Breaks*.

12

KELLY'S STORY

MARK O'HALLORAN

Interior. Small bedroom. Morning.
The small bedroom of a council house in the midlands of Ireland. It
is a crystal-bright winter's morning. Light pours in through a square
window, which is clouded with condensation or fern-frost, its frame
edged with cheap curtain. The room itself is drab and functional. On
a single bed and under blankets is a twenty-one-year-old woman.
This is KELLY. KELLY *presents herself to the world as being comical*
or absurd, but beneath this she is serious and thoughtful. She wakes
and, with effort, rolls herself to sitting. Her long hair hangs shapeless
from a centre parting. She is short and heavy-set. She sits a moment,
ill and cold, kneading her stomach.

Interior. Small bathroom. Morning.
KELLY, *in pyjamas, is kneeling before a toilet bowl, holding*
her hair back from her face. She leans forward and retches. Her
stomach holds only bile, which she spits into the bowl. She rests
back on her hunkers and takes some toilet tissue. A female voice is
heard from elsewhere in the house.
KELLY'S MOTHER (*voiceover*). Kelly!
KELLY *wipes her mouth and throws the tissue in the bowl.*

KELLY (*shouting off*). I'm up!

KELLY *rises, flushes the toilet and then rinses her mouth.*

Interior. Small kitchen. Morning.

KELLY *is in the kitchen putting her green coat on over a garish skirt and jumper combo. She quickly gulps down tea. Her* MOTHER, *a heavy-set woman, forty-six, sits at the table, watching. A third female,* KELLY's *sister* CLAIRE, *sixteen, is also in the room. Claire has obvious special needs.*

KELLY'S MOTHER (*to* KELLY). Why you not eating?

KELLY (*with displeasure*). Fucken Janet's picking me up. I'm late.

KELLY'S MOTHER. If she annoys you that much, go in on your scooter.

KELLY. Too far, I'd freeze. Bye, Claire.

She kisses CLAIRE *on the head.*

CLAIRE. Yeah.

KELLY *then kisses her* MOTHER *on the cheek.*

KELLY'S MOTHER. I hate that jumper on you.

KELLY. I know. It makes me laugh.

KELLY *goes.*

Exterior. Council estate. Morning.

KELLY *sits on a low wall on the edge of the estate, smoking. She is dressed in her green coat with mismatched jumper, skirt and coloured tights. On her head is a faux-fur hat in the shape of a small animal. She sits, waiting for her lift, looking troubled and almost comical.*

Interior. Car. Morning.

KELLY *is in the passenger seat of* JANET's *Toyota Yaris.* JANET, *twenty-three, is a slim, dark haired, woman who wears too much make-up. She is something of a gossip. They drive through a bleak landscape.* KELLY *watches bog and field as it passes. She doesn't feel like conversing and is still unwell.*

JANET. How's the radio station working out?

(*No reply.*)

Meet anyone famous yet?

KELLY (*with attitude*). In fucken Athlone?!

JANET *is hardly pleased with* KELLY's *tone. They settle.*

JANET. I seen Shauna Blake out Thursday night, wall-falling.

(*Small beat.*)

Must have been children's allowance night.

KELLY. Fuck sake!

KELLY *turns the radio up loud.* JANET *is annoyed by this.*

JANET. What? I not allowed say nothing?

KELLY. Not pure fucken slander, anyways.

JANET *turns the radio right back down.*

JANET. And this is my fucking car, too, let me remind you.

KELLY. I pay you twenty quid a week for the pleasure.

JANET. Well, you can fuck off in future.

KELLY. Fine.

KELLY *turns the radio back up to the max and looks out the window, ill.* JANET *is clearly raging.*

Exterior. Car. Morning.

JANET *has pulled up at an isolated spot.* KELLY *is out of the car, being ill on the verge.* KELLY's *hat is on the ground.* JANET *stands nearby. She eventually bends down and picks up the hat for* KELLY. *She is delighted at the spectacle.*

Interior. Office. Day.

The small, open-plan office of a community radio station. There are ten work desks set out in the space with sound studios off. A large window looks out to the back of a dreary town. The workforce is made up, for the most part, of young interns and researchers.

KELLY *sits at her desk, isolated and ill. Some numbing jingles from the radio broadcast fill the office.*

Interior. Office toilet. Day.
KELLY, *in a cubicle, has been ill again. She wipes her mouth and her eyes. She stands, exhausted.*
KELLY (*low to herself*). Fucking hell.
She fixes herself as best she can and leaves.

Interior. Kitchen. Noon.
KELLY *is in the small office kitchen. She looks worn. The clock says 12.45. She empties a soup sachet into a mug and sets the kettle to boil. A young man enters. This is COLM, twenty-three. He wears a dark hoodie and is almost handsome. They edge around one another as he throws a teabag in a cup. He comes to lean against a counter. They wait for the kettle. KELLY holds her mug. If she could think of anything to say, she would. COLM looks at her and eventually speaks.*
COLM. You new, no?
KELLY. On placement. Part time.
KELLY *smiles, self-conscious, and looks down at her mug. The kettle edges toward boiling. She tries to make an effort.*
KELLY (*continued*). Having this cuppa soup, shite.
KELLY *laughs low and looks down again. This unexpectedly dissolves into a wave of emotion she can't halt. She struggles not to cry. COLM is unsure what is happening.*
COLM. You OK?
KELLY. I, no, I fucken...
KELLY *tries to swallow down her emotion and accidentally lets slip her mug. It falls and smashes. She stands, upset and helpless. She leaves.*

Exterior. Laneway. Day.

A laneway behind the office building. KELLY *is sitting on a pallet near to a skip and a side door. She is trying to pull herself together and smokes with unsteady hands.* COLM *arrives out and finds her. He is unsure what to say.*

COLM. Something I said?

She looks up and splutters a messy laugh. He stands, bemused.

KELLY. Not that, no.

COLM. What so?

She looks at him. He stands, kindly, confused, and she may almost feel sorry for him. She needs to confess.

KELLY. Probably pregnant, I think. That's all.

He has no idea how to respond to this. She laughs low. COLM *struggles to be helpful.*

COLM. You want me to go in and get one of the girls?

KELLY. I do in my hole. They'd love this.

He laughs, as does KELLY. *Beat. He speaks low and serious.*

COLM. You done a test?

KELLY. Can't afford one til I'm paid.

COLM. So what makes you think, so?

KELLY. I'm sick half the day and fucken mental the rest.

She tries to laugh but looks down at her feet again, hopeless. COLM *stays looking at her and decides on something.*

COLM. I can get you a pregnancy thing, if you want, out of the pharmacy. Put your mind at rest.

(*No reply.*)

You can pay me back, then.

(*No reply.*)

Do it round at my place, even, if you want, for privacy. I live in a shithole across the diamond.

She laughs.

COLM (*continued*). That a weird thing to offer?

She giggles some more. She looks up at him.

KELLY. Yes. Nice, though.

KELLY *rises, puts out her cigarette and wipes her skirt.*

KELLY (*continued*). Fuck my life, I reckon.

She looks at him a moment longer.

KELLY (*continued*). You don't has to do this.

COLM. I know that.

(*Small beat.*)

We go?

She decides to go with him and they leave.

Interior. Bathroom. Day.

KELLY *stands in* COLM's *bathroom and sets about removing the pregnancy test from its packaging. She then takes down her tights and knickers awkwardly and sits on the toilet. She manoeuvres the pregnancy test into position and pisses on it.*

Interior. Living room. Day.

KELLY *is back in the living room. She has the pregnancy-test stick with her. She places it down on the coffee table to await the result.*

COLM *watches her and fakes a sort of comedic incredulity.*

COLM. Did you just after piss on that and put it on my table?

KELLY. It has a cap goes back on, it's clean.

She laughs and sits. She seems more animated.

KELLY (*continued*). You must think I'm a pig.

COLM. How long does it take?

KELLY. I haven't a notion. Five minutes, maybe.

She is searching in her coat pocket for cigarettes.

KELLY (*continued*). Can I smoke? You want one?

COLM. Go on.

She offers him one and he accepts. She then goes about lighting them. Her hand shakes slightly as she reaches the lighter flame towards his mouth.

KELLY. My hands.

(*Small beat.*)

I hardly knows you. I don't.

(*Small beat.*)

What's your name?

COLM. Colm.

KELLY. Nice to meet you, fucken hell.

She laughs at the situation. They smoke. They wait.

COLM. There a fella involved?

She looks at him undecided and toys with her cigarette. A sort of honesty descends.

KELLY. No.

(*Small beat.*)

A one-night what-ya-call, a mistake.

COLM. Right.

Beat. She worries she's being judged. She smokes and looks towards him.

KELLY. You're thinking, like, you're looking at me now.

COLM. No.

Beat. She smokes.

KELLY. Met him at this stupid disco, organised, we'd all went to, in fucking Cavan. A Goth, an emo lad, and he...

(*Unexpected emotion.*)

I was drunk and he starts kissing me then and I'm not used to that, so... He had a flat.

Beat. She goes further.

KELLY (*continued*). During all the cold, this was, before Christmas.

(*She remembers.*)

The lake even was froze over next morning, I remember. The whole country like some fucking miracle, all silver.

(*Beat.*)

He was nice, actually. Texted me a few times.
(*Beat.*)
Don't know why I'm telling you all this.
Beat. She looks towards the coffee table.
KELLY (*continued*). Should I look?
COLM. Is it ready?
KELLY. I don't know.
Small beat. She seems almost frozen for a moment.
COLM. What will you do if it says whatever?
She smiles, more vulnerable than she realises.
KELLY. Might go to England. Get rid of it.
COLM. Right.
KELLY. If I can find the fucken money together.
She looks at him, as if for assurance or rebuke.
KELLY (*continued*). I don't even know you. Talking like this. You could sink me.
(*Changing subject.*)
This cigarette tastes rank.
She puts it out and stands. She advances on the table where the test stick is. She picks it up without looking at it yet.
KELLY (*continued*). Here goes nothing.
She checks the result. She laughs or inhales short. She looks at him. The words almost stick.
KELLY (*continued*). Yeah. It's a yeah. I am.
Beat. She covers her mouth and hides her emotion.
COLM. You OK?
Silent beat. She recovers herself. She holds the pregnancy test up and looks at him, faking nonchalance.
KELLY. Can I throw this out?
COLM. There's a bin in the kitchen.
KELLY. Bingo.
She traipses off.

Interior. Building. Day.

COLM *and* KELLY *make their way up the back stairs, slowly, to the open-plan office.* KELLY *is more than a little jangled.*

KELLY. I'll go look see websites or that, for England. What arrangements, maybe.

COLM. Take my workstation.

KELLY. Yeah?

COLM. The screen faces the wall. No one be able to see what you're looking at, that way.

This affects her. They reach their landing. She deflects.

KELLY. I'm fucking starving now. Off tomorrow, anyways. You're nice.

She kisses him on the cheek. They enter the office.

Interior. Office. Day.

KELLY *is at* COLM's *workstation. It is close to a corner and angled to the wall. The life of the open-plan office goes on around her. She is looking up sites for information on abortion services in the UK or support networks in Ireland. She jots down phone numbers and eyes her colleagues to make sure she is not being seen.*

Exterior. Council house. Afternoon.

KELLY *is by the side of her family home. She stands a moment as the evening closes in. It is not yet dark and she looks out at a tangle of urban fields and the backs of houses.*

With some difficulty, she wheels her battered scooter to the front of the house. She gets on and cranks it into spluttering life. There is something ridiculous about her on this vehicle, but she is not bothered.

We watch her as she rides through the estate and out to other parts of the small grim town; streets and laneways.

Interior. Fast-food restaurant. Late afternoon.

KELLY *sits alone at a table in a local chipper. A flicker of neon and pop music. She sits to a meal of chips etc. She seems numb and detached. She takes out the paper that she jotted phone numbers on earlier and looks at it. There are other customers about, but she doesn't acknowledge them.*

Interior. Sitting room. Late afternoon.

KELLY *is sitting on a couch in a sparse, grim front room in a council house. A window looks out to a bleak urban landscape beyond. There is another young woman sitting nearby. This is* SHAUNA, *twenty-one. She is pretty but hard-looking. A three-year-old toddler,* JAMIE, *plays nearby. There is a sort of unspoken awkwardness between the two women as they strain for conversation.* SHAUNA *looks as if she has just woken.*

SHAUNA. We was down sleeping when you knocked. He has his nap.

KELLY. He's gone pure big.

SHAUNA. Loves his eating.

They both look at the child playing and a silence opens.

SHAUNA (*continued*). I never knew you was home. You finish your course?

KELLY. Only just.

SHAUNA. I thought you'd move to Dublin.

KELLY. I will.

SHAUNA. Exactly.

Beat. SHAUNA *looks at* KELLY *and perceives a worry.*

SHAUNA (*continued*). You're quiet. You seem something. You OK?

KELLY. Yeah.

(*Beat.*)

I called only 'cause I was talking about you today with Janet Caughlan.

SHAUNA. Which one's she?

KELLY. She was part of the Youthreach crowd.

SHAUNA. They was mostly Karl's friends.

KELLY. She's a fucking viper, anyways.

SHAUNA. They all are, this town.

Long beat. SHAUNA *decides to say something.*

SHAUNA (*continued*). Karl's gone. You know that?

KELLY. My mam said.

SHAUNA. Yeah?

KELLY. Where'd he go?

SHAUNA. Moved to England.

KELLY. Right.

Beat.

SHAUNA. Gone six months. Hardly hear from him. Rings sometimes, though, when he's blocked. Saying he loves Jamie, misses him and asking me to wake the child, to put him on the fucking phone, the middle of the night, like. Lovely.

(*Small beat.*)

He doesn't give a fuck about us, anyways. Never sends money nor nothing, no.

She rises. Small beat.

SHAUNA. I get vexed. Here on my own, like.

She may be crying but is contained. She looks at JAMIE. *Beat.*

SHAUNA. I'll put on the kettle, will I? You want a sandwich or something?

KELLY. The size of me.

SHAUNA. You look good. Wait for me, anyways.

SHAUNA *leaves the room.* KELLY *and* JAMIE *are left.* KELLY *looks at the child. He plays away, oblivious.*

Interior. Council house. Evening.

KELLY *is in the kitchen with her* MOTHER. *It is dark outside. They dry dishes.* KELLY *watches her* MOTHER *close. Eventually.*

KELLY. I thought maybe you and me might go for a drink tomorrow night.

KELLY'S MOTHER. Why?

KELLY. Why not? We never.

KELLY'S MOTHER. With Mike?

KELLY. No. Just me and you just.

Her MOTHER *looks at her, quizzically, a moment.* KELLY *puts some dishes away.* CLAIRE *calls inaudibly from elsewhere in the house and catches her* MOTHER's *attention.*

KELLY'S MOTHER. Hold on.

(*Calling off.*)

What?

KELLY'S MOTHER *leaves.* KELLY *continues to dry the dishes and looks out the back window to the darkness beyond.*

Interior. Council house. Evening.

KELLY *is in the sitting room of her family home. She sits on a couch watching television. Beside her is* CLAIRE. CLAIRE *has her arms around* KELLY. KELLY'S MOTHER *and stepfather,* MIKE, *are here also and are drinking cans of beer.*

Interior. Small bedroom. Night.

KELLY *lies in her bed. It is late. She is not sleeping.*

Interior. Shopping centre. Day.

KELLY *sits on a bench in a small-town shopping centre. It is not particularly busy but populated with older people and young women with prams.* KELLY *has a sandwich and picks at it, nauseous. Life goes on around her.*

Exterior. Town. Day.

KELLY *buzzes through the small town on her scooter.*

Interior. House. Evening.

KELLY *is in the kitchen of her family home. She is ready to go out and waits on her* MOTHER. *Her stepfather,* MIKE, *and* CLAIRE *are at the table.* KELLY *may be nervous but is covering.*

KELLY (*meaning her* MOTHER). The fuck is she?

MIKE. Dolling herself up.

Beat. KELLY *watches* MIKE *and* CLAIRE.

KELLY. You all right being left here, Mike?

MIKE. Claire can mind me.

(CLAIRE *smiles.*)

I has some cans in, anyways.

Some noise from the hallway. KELLY *readies herself.*

KELLY. There's her.

She exits.

Interior. Pub. Evening.

KELLY'S MOTHER *is at a low table in a half-enclosed smoking area at the back of a small pub.* KELLY *delivers a pint of lager to her* MOTHER *and has a Lucozade for herself. A gas heater hisses nearby but they keep their coats on.* KELLY *sits and tries masking her nervousness. Her* MOTHER *has an idea why she's been asked here and sits, flinty.*

KELLY'S MOTHER. What you drinking?

KELLY. Lucozade.

(*Her* MOTHER *makes a face.*)

I like it.

KELLY'S MOTHER. I think it tastes like sick.

KELLY. Thanks.

Small beat.

KELLY'S MOTHER. You cold?

KELLY. I has my coat on.

KELLY'S MOTHER. Still.

Long beat. There is a tension between them. KELLY *can't meet her* MOTHER'S *eyes. She looks at a set of keys on the table.*

KELLY. I hate this fucking town.

KELLY'S MOTHER. What's that to do with anything?

KELLY. Nothing.

Beat. KELLY'S MOTHER *shifts and looks hard at her daughter.*

KELLY'S MOTHER (*low*). You got something to say?

KELLY. In a while.

Beat. KELLY *edges toward upset. Her* MOTHER *stays focused.*

KELLY'S MOTHER. What?

KELLY. Wait.

KELLY'S MOTHER. Look at me.

KELLY *doesn't look up. She fidgets with a beer mat now.*

KELLY'S MOTHER (*continued*). I'm not stupid.

KELLY. I know that.

KELLY'S MOTHER. Well, say it out, so. Be done.

KELLY *slowly begins to scratch and sunder the beer mat. She feels pinned. Eventually.*

KELLY'S MOTHER (*continued; low and direct*). You pregnant?
No reply.

KELLY'S MOTHER (*continued*). Kelly?

KELLY. Sorry.

KELLY'S MOTHER. So.

Beat. KELLY'S MOTHER *is disturbed or emotional.* KELLY *reaches for her cigarettes.*

KELLY. You want a smoke?

KELLY'S MOTHER. How far along?

Small beat. KELLY *draws a cigarette from her packet and looks down at it. She turns it in her fingers.*

KELLY. Nine weeks, ten weeks.

KELLY'S MOTHER. Jesus Christ.

Beat. KELLY'S MOTHER*'s mood darkens.*

KELLY'S MOTHER (*continued*). I thought you had sense.

KELLY. I do.

KELLY'S MOTHER. Then how the fuck? Why?

KELLY. I done a mistake. It was nothing.

Small beat.

KELLY'S MOTHER (*almost to herself*). Your college and your course?

Silence. Her MOTHER *lifts and lights a cigarette.* KELLY *may cry. She trembles slightly as she lights her own.*

KELLY'S MOTHER (continued). So what now, so?

KELLY. I don't know.

Beat.

KELLY (*continued*). I mightn't keep it.

KELLY'S MOTHER. What does that mean?

KELLY. Get rid of it with an abortion.

KELLY'S MOTHER. Kelly.

Beat.

KELLY'S MOTHER (*continued*). You don't has to. Look at me. We can help.

KELLY. How?

KELLY'S MOTHER. There's me and Mike. Isn't it?

KELLY. Mam.

KELLY'S MOTHER. Your father, even?

KELLY. I'm not calling him.

Beat. KELLY *stares down at the table.*

KELLY'S MOTHER. You talked to anyone even?

KELLY. Like who?

KELLY'S MOTHER. Like a doctor. Like someone.

KELLY. No.

KELLY'S MOTHER. No.

(*Beat.*)

You'll need to. I'll organise. Look up at me, I said.

KELLY. Sorry.

A customer makes their way to the smoking area to light up. The place is too small for the conversation to continue and silence spreads. Beat. KELLY stands.

KELLY (*continued*) I need the toilet.

She leaves.

Interior. Pub toilet. Night.

The cubicle of a pub toilet. KELLY, still clothed, sits resting on the toilet. The cubicle is almost like a cell. She cries.

Interior. Car. Morning.

It is a bright winter. KELLY and her MOTHER drive towards Dublin. KELLY looks out of the window at the passing countryside and the beginnings of the city. She and her MOTHER do not talk.

Interior. Well Woman clinic. Afternoon.

KELLY *and her* MOTHER *are in a small office in the Well Woman clinic. A* COUNSELLOR *has information sheets ranged across a table and is going through various options.* KELLY *sits mostly silent.*

COUNSELLOR. The clinic in Liverpool caters for lots of Irish and even provides a special price for girls who travel from the Republic. They do both medical and surgical abortion. With a medical abortion after ten weeks it can involve a stay over in Liverpool of anything from three to five days.

KELLY'S MOTHER. She'd never afford that.

COUNSELLOR. The surgical procedure, then, is typically done under general anaesthetic. The operation itself is completed in five to ten minutes.

KELLY'S MOTHER. So over and back the same day?

COUNSELLOR. That's common. It might be advisable to do a

Imagery and design used by the Abortion Rights Campaign, an organisation that has been at the forefront of the movement for reproductive rights in Ireland. They are also the organisers of the annual March for Choice demonstrations.

One of many DIY apparel fundraising initiatives was born out of a banner design for a pro-choice march made by architect and designer, Rae Moore.

HunReal Issues is a grassroots campaign to inform young women in Ireland about reproductive rights and provide an opportunity for people to engage with conversations and activism around reproductive rights. Founded by Andrea Horan, its logo and brand identity was designed in collaboration with Sarah Fox.

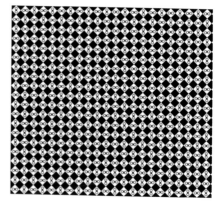

Repeal badges and imagery designed by Niall Sweeney

Ailbhe Smyth by Becky Butler, image courtesy of Repeal Project and Anna Cosgrave

The Repeal Project, by Anna Cosgrave, gained huge traction with its simple black and white design. The 'Repeal' jumpers became massively popular, making it almost impossible to walk down a street in an Irish city, or through a crowd at a festival, without spotting the now iconic design. The Repeal Project has also produced portraits, videos and events all geared towards advocating for the repeal of the Eighth Amendment, and has been seen as a visually galvanising force in the movement.

Tropical Popical is a nail bar in Dublin, Ireland

Speaking of IMELDA Opening (unofficially) the St Patrick's Day Parade
in London with a pro-choice poem, 2017

Kiki Na Art is handcrafted jewelery by Dubliner Ciarna Pham. The one-off bespoke pieces here celebrate female empowerment and bring attention to the issue of reproductive rights.

Banners from the Artists' Campaign
to Repeal the Eighth Amendment

OUR TOIL DOTH SWEETEN OTHERS

Photograph by Christian Kerskens, Artists' Campaign Banners by Alice Maher, Rachel Fallon, Breda Mayock, Aine Phillips and Sarah Cullen

stay over in the city, just in case, but most people don't. I have information booklets here with prices and contact details for that clinic. It's probably the cheapest option.

KELLY'S MOTHER. No grant available, no help?

COUNSELLOR. None.

KELLY'S MOTHER. They'd hate to make it easy on the girls.

KELLY *has collected the booklets.*

COUNSELLOR. Now, I am legally obliged to go through all of the other options open to you, OK?

KELLY'S MOTHER. Thanks.

The COUNSELLOR *begins to lay out some other fact sheets.* KELLY *and her* MOTHER *sit silent.* KELLY *holds the Liverpool details in her hands.*

Interior. Shopping centre. Day.

KELLY *and her* MOTHER *sit in a bright modern shopping centre in Dublin's city centre. They both eat small tubs of ice cream. Her* MOTHER *looks at her, concerned.*

KELLY'S MOTHER. You won't get sick all that in the car, I hope.

KELLY *smiles. She is comfortable here in her* MOTHER's *care.*

Interior. Council house. Afternoon.

KELLY, MIKE *and her* MOTHER *are in the small kitchen. They sit at the table. The leaflets are on the tabletop before them and they are discussing* KELLY's *possibilities.*

KELLY'S MOTHER. We can put your name on the housing list. Get you someplace here around.

Beat.

KELLY. I don't want that. I'd go mad.

KELLY'S MOTHER. Why? I'm here. I'll help.

KELLY. You have Claire.

KELLY'S MOTHER. We'll do our best.

Beat.

KELLY. I don't want to stay around here. This estate.

KELLY'S MOTHER. Why?

KELLY. 'Cause if I do I'll go rotten; I'll go mad. Like all the rest of them others. Nothing.

KELLY'S MOTHER. Like me, is it?

Small beat.

KELLY. No.

Beat. A silence hangs. KELLY *decides to speak.*

KELLY (*continued*). When I was younger. When half the girls on this estate was practically... Shauna Blake and Keelan fucken O'Meara. Fourteen and fifteen years old. Off riding married men behind of the factory. I wasn't one of them. I'm not.

Beat.

KELLY (*continued*) I done one mistake.

MIKE (*to* KELLY'S MOTHER). You never brought her up to stay around here, did you?

KELLY'S MOTHER. I know that.

MIKE. So?

Beat. No one wishes to speak.

MIKE (*continued*). How much it cost?

KELLY. Four hundred and fifty English.

MIKE. Including flights?

KELLY. No.

(*As if to offer hope.*)

I can sell my scooter.

Beat. KELLY's MOTHER *rises and goes to the sink.*

MIKE (*to* KELLY'S MOTHER). Well?

Beat. KELLY'S MOTHER *stands looking and then decides to speak.*

KELLY'S MOTHER. It's not abortion I care about. I don't give a fuck about that. It's you I care about.

KELLY. I know.

Beat.

MIKE. So?

Beat

KELLY'S MOTHER. I can cover the price of two flights.

KELLY. You going to come with me?

KELLY'S MOTHER. Hardly leave you off on your own, can I?

Small beat.

KELLY'S MOTHER (*continued*). I'll talk to my sister Christina. She'll lend us the rest.

(*Small beat.*)

Been through similar herself.

Beat.

MIKE. Is that decided?

(*No reply. To* KELLY.) Kelly?

KELLY. Mam?

Beat.

KELLY'S MOTHER. Go on.

MIKE (*to* KELLY). Well, book what needs booking, so.

KELLY *stands and takes her phone. She exits. Her mother is upset.*

Exterior. Town. Afternoon.
KELLY *is on her scooter and moving through the town.*

KELLY *is at a small newsagent and placing a 'For Sale' about her scooter on a community noticeboard.*

Interior. Office. Day.
KELLY *is at work. She is at her desk.* COLM *passes. She smiles at him. He nods a cursory hello and is gone.*
Interior. House. Night.
KELLY *lies in bed, awake.*

Exterior. House. Day.

KELLY *is round the side of her house. There is a* YOUNG MAN *with her. She is showing him her scooter in the hopes of selling it. He is a slim young man in his late teens. He is giving close inspection to the vehicle.*

KELLY. You can have it for one-twenty.

YOUNG MAN. What horsepower is she?

KELLY. How the fuck would I know?

Beat. The YOUNG MAN *straightens up.*

YOUNG MAN. I'll give you eighty.

Small beat.

KELLY. Can't take less than a hundred. I'm saving up for an abortion.

The YOUNG MAN *thinks this is a great joke.*

YOUNG MAN. Deal, so.

They shake on it.

Exterior. House. Late Afternoon.

The night is falling. KELLY *stands at the back of the house. Her scooter is gone. She watches the light fade.*

Interior. House. Early morning.

KELLY *sits on the side of her bed looking at the window.*

Interior. House. Early morning.

KELLY *and her* MOTHER *are in the kitchen. They have had breakfast. It is still dark outside. Her* MOTHER *is putting a few items into a small holdall.*

KELLY'S MOTHER. You sick?

KELLY. I'm all right. My stomach just.

KELLY'S MOTHER *closes up the bag.*

KELLY'S MOTHER. I has a new nightie for you, inside. And some extra knicks.

KELLY *watches her* MOTHER *a moment and then out of the window where the first dawn light can be perceived.*

Interior. Airport. Morning.
KELLY *and her* MOTHER *are at their boarding gate. There are a number of young women here too. One in particular catches* KELLY'S MOTHER's *eye. She is a young girl of eighteen, slight and nervous. She is on her own.*
KELLY'S MOTHER (*to* KELLY. *Low*). That young one over. I bet.
KELLY. Mam.
KELLY'S MOTHER. I'm only looking.
The flight is about to be called. People stand to get in line. KELLY *is about to rise. Her* MOTHER *holds her arm.*
KELLY'S MOTHER (*continued*). Wait. Listen. Stop.
(KELLY *sits again.*)
Just cause the money is spent, just cause, means nothing, all right? If you want to change your mind, change your mind. I don't care, I don't give a fuck, even. All right?
KELLY. I know.
The flight is called. A moment. They both stand.

Interior. Taxi. Morning.
Liverpool airport. KELLY *and her* MOTHER *get in to a taxi at the airport. The* DRIVER *is a middle-aged male and is friendly.*
DRIVER. Morning, ladies.
KELLY. Hello.
DRIVER. Where can I take you to, then?
The DRIVER *has already begun to move towards the airport exit.* KELLY'S MOTHER *hands him a piece of paper with the address on it.*

KELLY'S MOTHER. There's an address there. I can't pronounce the road it's on.

The DRIVER *takes the piece of paper.*

KELLY. It's the BPAS clinic.

The DRIVER *knows exactly where they are talking about. His demeanour changes totally. He goes silent. They travel. He looks at them in the rear-view mirror. This bothers* KELLY'S MOTHER *greatly. She speaks.*

KELLY'S MOTHER (*to the* DRIVER). You all right?

DRIVER. Pardon?

KELLY'S MOTHER. 'Cause if you're going to be judging us, you can let us out here.

DRIVER. I got no problem, love.

KELLY'S MOTHER. Good, so.

The journey continues. KELLY'S MOTHER *is clearly furious.* KELLY *looks out of the window at the passing city.*

Exterior. BPAS clinic, Liverpool. Morning.

KELLY *and her* MOTHER *are outside the clinic. It looks more like a large Victorian townhouse then a medical facility. They are waiting to be admitted.*

Interior. BPAS clinic, Liverpool. Morning.

KELLY *and her* MOTHER *are in the clinic, at a screened-off cash desk.* KELLY'S MOTHER *counts out and pays over the £400 for the procedure.*

Interior. BPAS clinic, Liverpool. Morning.

KELLY *and her* MOTHER *are in a large, sterile waiting area. They both seem nervous.* KELLY *is filling out an assessment form on a clipboard. There are three other young women present. The young girl from Dublin airport is one of them.*

KELLY'S MOTHER (*to the young woman*). We seen you at the airport this morning.

YOUNG WOMAN (*hesitant*). Oh?

KELLY'S MOTHER. You here on your own?

YOUNG WOMAN. My sister was going to be here, but she couldn't.

KELLY'S MOTHER. Where you from?

KELLY. Mam.

(*To young woman.*)

She'd talk to anyone.

A nurse enters.

NURSE. Kelly.

KELLY *rises. Her* MOTHER, *too. She hands* KELLY *the small bag.*

KELLY'S MOTHER. There. Your nightdress, I said.

KELLY. Yeah.

KELLY'S MOTHER. You OK? You sure?

KELLY. Yeah.

KELLY'S MOTHER *hugs her and fixes her hair, emotional.*

KELLY'S MOTHER (*low*). I love you. Yes, and I'll get a sandwich and a drink for when you're finished.

KELLY. Thanks.

She goes. Her MOTHER *collects herself. She looks at the other girls.*

Interior. Clinic. Day.

KELLY *is on an examination table. There is a* PRACTITIONER *nearby. She is about to scan* KELLY'S *belly.*

PRACTITIONER. After this scan we'll send you through for the procedure, OK?

KELLY. Yes.

PRACTITIONER. Lie back.

The PRACTITIONER *applies gel to* KELLY'S *exposed tummy.* KELLY *watches her work.*

KELLY. Is it OK if I don't see the scan?

PRACTITIONER. I have the monitor turned away.

KELLY. Thanks.

KELLY *lies back.*

Interior. Clinic. Day.

KELLY *is in a small changing area. She is pulling her nightdress on over her head and fixes it. Beat. She then realises something and leans down and takes off her knickers. She almost laughs at her own stupidity.*

She is now in a smaller waiting area with three other women. Silence.

Interior. Clinic. Day.

KELLY *is on a small operating table. Her legs are placed in stirrups. She is lying back and being prepped. A female ANAESTHETIST is there to administer a general anaesthetic. She is looking for a vein on* KELLY'*s arm and is having difficulties. She is kind, professional and caring.*

ANAESTHETIST. Just looking for a vein, darling.

KELLY. I'm probably too fat.

ANAESTHETIST. You're fine.

The nurse continues. Beat.

KELLY. I thought I'd be upset, this bit.

ANAESTHETIST. You not like needles?

KELLY. No, not that. Just the whole other, I was afraid.

ANAESTHETIST. Yeah?

KELLY. That I'd feel rotten and stop. That I'd change my mind. Only I don't.

The nurse finds a vein.

ANAESTHETIST. There we are. Now. I want you to count backwards from ten. OK?

KELLY. Will this put me to sleep?
ANAESTHETIST. Try.
KELLY. Ten, nine… eight…
She is going and then gone.

Interior. Clinic. Day.
KELLY *is lying back on a bed surrounded by screens. She wakes, innocent. A* WARD NURSE *is passing. She sees* KELLY *is awake.*
WARD NURSE. You're awake?
KELLY. I think.
WARD NURSE. Sit up. That's it. You feel all right?
KELLY. Yes.
WARD NURSE. Up you get, so to standing.
KELLY *stands.*
WARD NURSE (*continued*). Good girl. There's a small kitchen over there with biscuits and tea. You should try eat something before you leave. Take your time. I'll get your mother.
KELLY. Thanks.
The WARD NURSE *goes.* KELLY *sits back down, groggy for a moment. There is a small flower pattern on her nightdress. She notices and looks at it, groggy.*

Interior. Clinic. Day.
KELLY *is in the small kitchen with her* MOTHER. *She is dressed and picks at the sandwich that her* MOTHER *got her.*
KELLY'S MOTHER. We'll have to go soon. There's only one bus takes us to the airport. We can't afford the taxi this time. You all right?
KELLY *doesn't stand yet.*

Interior. Bus. Day.
KELLY *and her* MOTHER *are on a bus to the airport.* KELLY

127

looks out at the city and its inhabitants. Her MOTHER *sits solemn beside her. She eventually turns to her daughter.*

KELLY'S MOTHER. I wonder how that other little one got on. Should we have waited and she alone?

KELLY. I don't know.

KELLY *turns to the window instead and watches the city slip by outside.*

Interior. Airport. Evening.

KELLY *and her* MOTHER *are at the airport waiting for their flight. They are silent. Her* MOTHER *eventually speaks.*

KELLY'S MOTHER. That's all done now. You leave all that here behind. OK?

KELLY. Yes.

KELLY'S MOTHER. I couldn't go through that all again.

The flight is announced. KELLY *stands. Outside on the runway the plane stands in the darkening evening.* KELLY *may find this moving.*

Exterior. Council estate. Morning.

A few days later. Early morning. KELLY *sits on a low wall, wearing her green coat and mismatched clothes. She has her hat on and smokes. She is waiting for her lift to work, alone.*

Mark O'Halloran is a writer and actor from Ennis, County Clare. Films he has written include *Adam & Paul*, *Garage* and *Viva*.

13

THE OBVIOUS EXPLANATIONS OF HOW POWER IS HELD AND EXERCISED OVER WOMEN ARE VERY BASIC

AILBHE SMYTH

Una Mullally: In late July 2017, Ailbhe Smyth, the lesbian, feminist, convener of the Coalition to Repeal the Eighth Amendment, LGBT rights activist and former head of Women's Studies at University College Dublin, sat in my kitchen and I asked her a few questions.

The first was reflecting on that thing foreign journalists asked us Irish folk in the aftermath of the marriage referendum.

How can Ireland have same-sex marriage and not abortion?
Ailbhe Smyth: For me, I always think that what it demonstrates very clearly is that the control of sexuality generally is very deeply rooted in our society, as it is in one shape or form in most societies. There is that want to control sexuality because it's what is 'wild' and will get out of control unless it's kept in check in some way or another, unless it's kept within institutions and conventions and boundaries and whatnot.

On one level that explains why gay, queer sexuality has always been so problematic and stigmatised and so marginalised, because that was a way of controlling it, keeping it on the outside, not letting it in. But even more fundamental than that is control of women's sexuality, women's reproduction. You go down through layers of power being exercised over people, layers of domination. And you actually come down to a kind of bedrock, which is that patriarchal society is founded on the control of women.

There are two, if not three, ways women are controlled; one is economically. The other one is, of course, through reproduction. Keeping ownership of and keeping hold of women who reproduce means keeping ownership of the products of that process. That, I think, goes very, very deep. Of course the third cornerstone – if you have can three cornerstones – of controlling women is through violence. So you have economic and reproductive control, and the exertion of physical and psychological force. These three dimensions of control seem to me to be interconnected. One feeds into the other. Single women in this country have always been frowned upon or treated as somewhat lesser people, and that's partly because they couldn't be controlled in the same way that 'married' women – that is to say reproductive women – could be controlled. I can hear *The Handmaid's Tale* in my own head as I'm saying this, because Margaret Atwood got that bit so right; that reproducing women had to be tightly held.

So you move through seeing a more gradual acceptance of people who are gay/queer, and finally it comes to a point where inevitably these people who are gay and lesbian – they're all sorts politically, they're all kinds – say, 'Hey, we'd like to have families. Everybody else gets married: why can't we?' What people are asking for in that seems incredibly radical, but it is in fact about saying, 'We've been outside for a long time, let us in because we want to do what you're doing, we want to do the same thing that you do.' So you get all the jokes, 'Why on earth would they want to get married? Do they not know what it's like?' and all that kind of thing. It's effectively a move towards inclusion, whereas I think where women say: 'We must and need to control our own bodies; we're not asking to be let into something; we're not asking to be included,' we are asking, or we are saying, that we need and must stand independently, separately, distinctively as ourselves, as people, as individuals and as collective groups. So it's not the same kind of political move and it doesn't come from the same sort of place. While there are very important and obvious connections between a referendum on same-sex marriage and having a referendum to give women the right to have an abortion, or simply to have control over their own pregnancies – which we don't have at the moment – more profoundly, there are, I think, some differences.

Is 'why don't we do what marriage equality did?' one of the things that you find people suggesting as an activist?
Yes, there is an enormous amount of really effective campaigning that we should learn from marriage equality and do as marriage equality did, and I hope we will be able to do that. But at the same time, you have to be able to recognise the different kinds challenges and obstacles there are. For this country at least, which has stayed somewhere back in the Middle Ages for longer than many of our European counterparts, women saying 'we control our own bodies, we control ourselves' is seen as very profoundly radical. And that is the separating out and moving away from forms of domination and ownership, because fundamentally that is women saying 'nobody owns my body'. We see that everywhere on the slogans – 'Get your rosaries off my

ovaries', that's 'nobody tells me what to do', 'I own myself' – that is all about saying we stand on our own two feet.

It's also why the national maternity policy has a clause in it that says actually the consent policy doesn't apply to women when they're pregnant because there are also the interests of the unborn involved. So a woman is never just herself. She can never just be there as herself – maybe connected with others through her family, friends and community and so on – but standing there as herself. Men don't have to go through that, whether they're gay or not. It's not to say there aren't huge difficulties for people who are gay, of course there are, but they are not quite the same problem. I think you go down another layer when you're looking at the control of women.

I think it's also probably true that you could apply and think about some of these matters when you're looking at attitudes towards trans people, because there, there is also a boundary crossing, doing something that is profoundly radical in the sense that people don't want you to move out of your box. 'We'll put you into our box – gay marriage – but we won't let you get out of another box,' which is also why we didn't have divorce until 1995. I was married in 1973, I was married for six months, and then we split, and we remained officially married until 1996, when we were able to get a divorce. That wasn't particularly in his interests, but it was absolutely that women had to be kept in their place, and that was inside a box, and generally a box called 'marriage'. What you have to do is produce all the children. It goes back layers and layers of history.

Sometimes I think that my explanation of it is very simplistic because it's so obvious, but often the obvious explanations of how power is held and exercised over women are very basic. Tell them what they can and can't do with their bodies, don't give them money – or very little, or control the amount they get – and if neither of these things work, there's always violence. I almost feel like apologising that that seems very basic and simple. It is very basic. It is very simple. And it's the one reason I keep hold of the word 'patriarchy'. It is still there in this country.

Think about the difficulties we went through for contraception, and the reason why, in the heel of the hunt, condoms became available in vending machines in the early 1990s – 1992, when the X Case[2] was going on – was because of the AIDS scare. It wasn't for women. The key move there was, obviously, we have to prevent the spread of AIDS, and quite rightly. But that wasn't actually thinking about what women need in order to control their lives, to some degree. None of us control our lives completely, but to have some degree of control over your lives, you need to be able to say when or if you want to reproduce. It's very, very basic.

---

[2] The X Case, 1992, was a landmark Irish Supreme Court case that established the right of Irish women to abortion if the life of the pregnant woman was at risk. The case involved a fourteen-year-old girl, known as 'X', who was raped by her neighbour and was suicidal. Before travelling for an abortion, the girl's family asked the Irish police (Garda Síochána) if DNA from the aborted foetus could be used as evidence in a court case against the neighbour who raped the girl. The Attorney General then sought and received an injunction against the girl travelling to have an abortion. This injunction, granted by the High Court, was appealed to the Supreme Court and overturned, establishing that a pregnant woman had a right to an abortion if there was a risk to her life, including suicide. The girl had a miscarriage shortly after the judgement was made. As for her attacker, he was convicted of statutory rape and sentenced to fourteen years although he only served three. In 2002 he was convicted of sexual assault and false imprisonment of a fifteen-year-old girl and received another prison sentence. The Supreme Court decision was only legislated for in July 2013 with the Protection of Life During Pregnancy Act.

Telling a woman she's going to be forced to reproduce, first of all by denying her contraception, and then when she's achieved access to that, by saying 'you'll never be able to have an abortion'; that's the most basic control you can think of.

I think back to 1983, about how very determined we were not to let that Eighth Amendment get into the constitution, and ultimately, despite the fact that 33 per cent voted against the Eighth being in the constitution, fundamentally we were powerless against forces that were greater than us, and those forces were the combined power of the State and the Catholic Church.

But it puzzles me that it has been so difficult and has taken us so long to get to this point with the Eighth Amendment again, despite everything that has happened. It puzzles me because we have had, and still have, a really vibrant, determined, clear-thinking and dedicated women's movement since the 1970s. But then I just think it shows you how incredibly powerful those patriarchal forces can be when they're massed against you. But the thing is, they need to be massed, and if you take away one element or you weaken one element, which is sort of the trick, then the whole superstructure weakens. So the Catholic Church has become very weak in this country over that time, and particularly since the early 1990s. Again, very much to do with sexuality, very much to do with clerical child sexual abuse, from the beginning of the 1990s, and also the abuse of power by male clerics over women having babies with them; making the women go ahead and have the babies and then the male clerics disown them, or hide them, or deal with them secretly. All of these things are in there in that mix. That was really the hook that began to rock the Catholic Church in this country.

You see that the weakening of the power of the Church in relation to the society as a whole, but specifically in relation to its collaboration with the State, has meant that what you're left with as a mass is the State, in a sense. And the State on its own is much weaker than the State and the Catholic Church. I don't know how well that holds up theoretically. The State has its institutions. The point about a State is that it's a many-headed thing and it's never a monolith. It was Foucault or someone who said that first, not me. There are many different aspects of the State, therefore there is always part of the State you can work on and work with. I think that's what marriage equality did. You can work with those things. But if it is in close collaboration with another major institution, like a religious institution, whether it's Catholicism or some other religion – it's not always Catholicism, in Northern Ireland it's both Protestantism and Catholicism, but it's still a strong religious base in the North with the State that's weak, which I think should give women in the North both something to hope for, and also something to be very wary of. We look as if we're in the same situation, but it's a very different setting. The State is more menaced and is on very different, less stable kind of grounds in the North. Whereas here, the State is actually pretty stable in the South, but the Church is on the shaky ground.

For all kinds of reasons, the Catholic Church has lost its role as a key authority in Ireland, and it won't ever regain it, certainly not in my lifetime or in yours. Precisely what will happen with religion in the contemporary world, I don't know, because there are other issues we have to cope with and confront and be honest about. But as an institution, the Catholic Church is fatally damaged.

What was the atmosphere like during the 1983 referendum campaign?
I missed all of the middle of the campaign. I was there at the

beginning and the end and was away for the middle; I was away for the year. I remember certainly at the beginning that we were very, very determined. Our resources were small and we didn't have that broad swathe of support there is now across Ireland much more generally.

In some ways it was quite a dangerous thing for people to do, to take on that Amendment campaign. To be against that Amendment, you were definitely putting yourself out there as somebody who – whatever your background – was a radical at the time. And while I think that people are very brave now, there is a broader baseline of support.

I think lots of people would simply laugh if you said to them [now], 'Well, you're being incredibly radical,' but I do recall for me personally it was absolutely the time when, in a way, I had to be very, very clear about what my politics were and what my principles were. My politics are absolutely feminist politics. My principles are absolutely feminist principles; that if we didn't have bodily autonomy and bodily integrity, we were not at the races, we were not getting anywhere with liberation.

I still cling on to women's liberation because that was so important to liberation, to do that and say it openly in the institution that I worked in in UCD [University College Dublin], I was seen as absolutely being incredibly radical. I would think, therefore, for every other woman and a lot of the men who put their heads above the parapet, it was the same.

I was a completely committed feminist; there was no question or doubt in my mind. But I had a daughter, I was still in a relationship with a man, I have a family. Really, it was profoundly shocking to so many of the people I knew. But I have to say it was also very shocking to them when I left my husband; it was very shocking when I had a child by another man; it was very shocking when I came out as lesbian in the late 1980s. All of these things were shocking! By that stage, when I came out as lesbian, frankly there was no one left to shock in my immediate environment.

I did feel, even at some very basic level, that to stand out and stand up for abortion in this country was a difficult thing to do, and yet it was very important. So I have vast unsurpassed admiration for the women and the men who fought all the way through that campaign. And when I came back – we didn't have Google or the internet and so on – it was just breathtaking to see how they held their ground. But the arguments tended to be quite theological arguments, very highly legalistic, and medical. And it was almost a technical discourse. You could be one or other of these experts: a lawyer, a medic, not many of us are theologians, but you could be one of those things. You were very rarely just standing there as a woman and saying: look, I'm not a theologian, I'm not a lawyer, I'm not a medic, I am a woman who has had an abortion and wants that to be legal and accessible and safe and free, or alternatively, that's a right I want to have, or I'm past childbearing age but it's something that I believe impinges on my personhood as woman, the fact that you deny me the right to control my own body.

It was incredibly divisive campaign. I remember in 1992 [the abortion referendum that followed the X Case] I was involved right the way through, and that was very bitter and divisive so, thinking back to 1983, it was even more so.

Now it is broadly seen that a woman speaking about her own experience and own needs is viewed as an 'expert' in a way women weren't viewed as 'experts' then, without being a lawyer or a doctor. That has been a big shift in the conversation. How would you characterise the way the atmosphere has changed over the last few years?

I think there are a number of things going on. First of all, there has always been pressure placed on women. I'm thinking back to 1992 specifically, because it was very difficult for women in 1982 or 1983 to say, 'I had an abortion,' although some very brave women, including Mary Holland, did, which was really quite extraordinary. I remember in 1992 it was particularly international journalists who would come over and say, 'We need to speak to women who have had an abortion,' and we used to say, 'We don't do wombs with a view,' because that's not actually what it's about, and that was very much about shielding and protecting women who had had abortions.

One of the reasons I think women are more willing to come forward is that we are more free. We are freer about sexuality and sex in Ireland than we were twenty-five or thirty years ago. There's no doubt about that. Two generations out there now grew up in a very different world, where being able to be at least more open about your sexuality and about your own sexual behaviour, your sex life, your partners and so on, is much more taken for granted than it used to be. That makes it easier to talk about personal experiences to do with abortion.

Linked to that, certainly for young women is: 'I have sex before I get married; I may never get married; I have sex and I have to be able to ensure that I don't end up with an unintended pregnancy.' There is that very common-sense, sensible, much more informed and educated approach to it, and also recognising that contraception goes wrong. There is that acceptance that having sex is not a bad thing, that having sex is a good thing, and it took us centuries to free ourselves from that notion, which was absolutely opposed by the Catholic Church.

It is a very confessional society, so there is a broader, more global dimension to it culturally or socially as a society, that telling your own story and laying down your experience as the basis for your understanding of life, so to speak, is quite powerful. That's a very powerful cultural strand in the 2000s much more generally. We saw that very clearly in the marriage equality referendum, where it was very difficult in the couple of years before the campaign to encourage couples to come out and speak, but once they did, it was almost like a snowball effect. People felt easier doing it because it was a more open society, because we're used to telling personal stories, because they're part of our culture, and I think that all has a knock-on effect on abortion.

We now have a real social movement, not just an organisation or a campaign or the Coalition. There is a social movement there now that goes across generations and across the country – maybe particularly in urban areas, nonetheless very present – where we challenge the society as a whole *not* to listen to our stories of abortion, because the stories have been kept so desperately secret, held so closely. I often think of the hearts where those secrets lie, and they could never be told, and that it's almost a provocation to people generally in this country to say: you know that there are secrets that have been buried. We know what happens when secrets are buried, whether it's Tuam,[3] whether it's the Magdalene Laundries, whether it's clerical sex abuse. We know this is rotten for society. It shows the rottenness of the foundations of the society. We don't want that any more. We don't want that kind of country. We don't want that kind of life. We don't live our lives like that any more. We live our

---

[3] Tuam is a town in County Galway and the location of the Bon Secours Mother and Baby Home. A local historian, Catherine Corless, spearheaded an investigation into the deaths of nearly 800 babies and children at the Home. A commission was established to investigate, and during excavations between November 2016 and February 2017, a large number of human remains were discovered. The investigation is ongoing at the time of writing.

lives more openly. We need society to listen and to hear those stories. I still think it's very difficult, because they are very intimate and personal stories. We don't generally speak about very intimate details in our lives. Why? Because they're intimate. We cherish our personal lives as well, particularly in a world where everything seems to be up for grabs and Instagrammable or whatever.

There are reasons why it can be still difficult for women. And also they know they're taking a risk. Twenty per cent of the population is still viscerally opposed to abortion. So, maybe their families don't know. Very likely they don't. I think of all of those secrets that are still there for women. We know that there are those secrets. I feel very sad when I think about that.

I think it is easier, but I don't think we should delude ourselves into thinking it's something you can just stand up and do. I don't think it's like that at all. There is part of me – and maybe it's my generation – that thinks we shouldn't have to. I wish we didn't have to. I wish women didn't have to stand up and talk in personal ways about very intimate things. And I ask myself, what is it about not just Ireland, but so much of contemporary culture and society, that means we can only be moved by personal stories? What has happened to reason and logic and right and justice and fairness and equality? That we need the emotional to move us? To change our minds and open up our thinking? I think that's an interesting question in itself, to which I, of course, don't have any answers.

For the past year I have just been amazed and delighted and thrilled and incredibly concerned that we manage, all of us in our glorious diversity, to work together for something that means so much for so many people and means so much for what this country is about. Because if we can't value women, we're not up to much; there is still that rottenness there at the base. I think there's tremendous, huge energy. I think it scatters off in so many brilliant, creative directions, and I think that will be a challenge for us in our campaigning when it comes to campaigning at referendum time. To hold all of that diverse and multicoloured creative and political energy, to hold that and present that to the people of Ireland – this is what this question of women's freedom and women's autonomy means. We call it abortion, but it is actually fundamentally about our freedom and our autonomy. So, because we're not allowed have abortion, that's the thing we have to name and fight for, in a way.

I know we can do it. I think it is going to be a great challenge. I'm hoping it will really give rise to what I think of as real, genuine conversations about what it means to be embodied as a woman, what it means to have that sense that you can make decisions about yourself, that you don't need and won't be dictated to by the State or by the Church or by anybody as to how you live your life. I think there will be very interesting conversations. I'm not thinking about divisiveness. I'm thinking about people in a very everyday way, and to see how that opens up the society to be much more honest and much more real. Abortion happens and it's never going to be stopped by constitutions and laws that restrict it. It's going to happen because contraception fails or because it isn't used or for whatever reason.

It seems to me that the energy is bubbling up. In the way that most political campaigns are about themselves and also about something else, it is about that desire for a country where young people think to themselves, 'We want a country we can believe in and a country we can trust.' Whether you call that the state or society, I want to live in a place where I am trusted, but also where I can feel I can trust it, so to speak. I think, therefore, it is about probably recalibrating a whole set of values that have been destabilised over the past thirty, forty years, destabilised by fairly intensive modernisation, technology, education, the collapse of the Catholic Church, and maybe a worry and a concern about how you actually form value systems in a world that moves so fast and is so profoundly unequal.

I object – and I will go on objecting until we remove it – to the existence of the Eighth Amendment in the constitution. I think it's probably time for us to have these kinds of conversations, which we started very effectively and successfully with the marriage equality referendum. But there's another layer, and that layer is about women and how women are treated and valued and how we matter.

Ailbhe Smyth is the convenor of the Coalition to Repeal the Eighth Amendment.

14

THE IMPORTANT THING IS THAT WE START A CONVERSATION

LISA McINERNEY

It is Gráinne who writes the story. Gráinne is not given to hard work or scholastic diligence and so even this act of writing is mildly scandalous. Gráinne is usually more interested in sniggering at a classmate's sincerity than in demonstrating sincerity of her own. Gráinne is more likely to spend the English class badgering the teacher for a toilet break, picking at the cuffs of her jumper, throwing little paper balls at the geeky girls (who are so easily embarrassed) and making an extravagant show of innocence when they snap around to face her. Gráinne has her pals. They are the kind of girls who smoke on the street outside the school. Otherwise she is unpopular but formidable and esteemed for that.

And so Ms Anna Walsh is surprised that the story, which lends itself so well to classroom discussion and provides such a solid framework for this unscheduled lesson on debate, has come from Gráinne. It is not particularly well written, but its subject is tackled with a rawness that might have been softened with the correct application of grammar and spelling and structure. It is, Ms Anna Walsh thinks briefly, almost experimental, a story that, if it came from an adult, might be lauded for its voice and authenticity. She briefly entertains the notion of taking it and passing it off as her own, submitting it to some literary journal in Dublin, winning praise for her fearless take on teenage sexuality and the point at which romance meets hard decision. Such a story to come from a girl like Gráinne, she marvels, in tandem with visions of accepting a prestigious award and a book deal. The most important thing for a teacher, she tells imaginary journalists, is to be completely open to the opinions and passions of your students. Teenage girls are capable of such incredible insight. They have such a sense of justice!

Gráinne's story is written in the first person. Its protagonist is a teenage girl whose best friend confides in her about an unplanned pregnancy. The protagonist is scared, but sisterly love is stronger than fear, and so she helps her friend arrange an abortion in Liverpool. The friends take the ferry over the Irish Sea. During the journey they have a run-in with a couple of mean girls who are skinny and stylishly dressed. In Liverpool they find the house they'll stay at, with the help of Google Maps. The nurses at the clinic are very nice. After the procedure, who do they meet at the clinic but the mean girls from the ferry. They feel no solidarity, but it's a sort of learning experience; snobby girls are no less in thrall to their fertility than sound girls. The friends realise they've shared a moment. They will keep the secret forever and be friends forever because of it.

Aifric is familiar with the story and is not surprised that Ms Walsh asked Gráinne to read it out in class. Aifric is studious and quiet. She has never liked Gráinne and has always been sure that Gráinne doesn't like her either. Gráinne seems to think that any display of intellect is nothing but showing off, that people do well at school only so they can lord it over people who do not. So it was a shock to Aifric when Gráinne asked her to read her story before she handed it in. She was looking for a smirk or some other sign of being had even as she took the pages from Gráinne. She read in a near-empty classroom with her best friend Jade beside her and Gráinne hovering with the other degenerates, Emily and Laura B, a row back and to the left.

'I really like it,' Aifric said, handing the pages back.

'You're only saying that,' Gráinne said.

'No, it's really good,' Aifric said, and knew that Gráinne had no way of knowing if she was being genuine, that the limits of the interaction had been set months or even years ago, when Gráinne decided she was cool and Aifric wasn't, when Gráinne surrendered any chance of there being honesty in their future conversations by becoming so sly and callous.

Aifric wonders now, as Gráinne reads and Ms Walsh leans, half smiling, against her desk with her arms folded and legs crossed, if Gráinne had asked her to read the story because she thought Aifric, so studious, so quiet, would baulk at the subject matter. Because she thought Aifric must be conservative, prudish, obedient, maybe even religious, or perhaps innocent instead, perhaps the kind of girl who didn't even know what abortion was, or that a girl had to go to Liverpool to procure one, certainly a virgin, certainly someone mightily afraid of a boy's body and ignorant as to the functions of her own. Now Aifric is annoyed. She listens to Gráinne read her story badly, stumbling over her words, unable to get a rhythm going, and is annoyed with herself too, for being pleased that Gráinne had asked for her opinion on the story before handing it in, for thinking that Gráinne might have done it out of respect for Aifric's story-writing aptitude. And, honestly, it is not a very good story. It's very unrealistic. There is barely any description in it. And it's boring. A story about two friends secretly leaving the country so one of them could have a procedure that was illegal at home – boring. How could you make that boring? Gráinne might thinks she's sharp and tough but, Aifric thinks, what she really is is a massive dope.

Jade is interested in everyone's reactions. Aifric had already told her about Gráinne's story, in the context of her being surprised that Gráinne had it in her to write something so current, and Jade shared that surprise, in the way Jade and Aifric share most of their opinions. Now Jade watches the faces of her classmates as Gráinne reads her story with a view to determining whether anyone is thinking what she's thinking: that maybe this is a super-personal story, in that Gráinne might have lived it, because, c'mon, she hasn't ever in her life shown any imagination prior to this so hey, join the dots, like. Jade looks particularly closely at Emily and Laura B to see if they show signs. Discomfort. Determination. Or tears, maybe? If it wasn't Gráinne, it was one of them, Jade thinks. Whose story is this? Imagine broadcasting it here. Like this. The absolute state. She sits and peers.

Gráinne finishes reading her story to encouraging murmurs, a couple of enunciated praise words. Ms Anna Walsh uncrosses her legs, stands, walks her unhurried, self-satisfied walk to the corner of the whiteboard, where she adopts that same cool pose.

'I think that this story is very important,' she says. 'Why do you think I think that?'

'Because Gráinne threatened to punch her in the tits if she didn't,' Molly whispers to Grace, who snorts, and so Ms Walsh turns first to her, her smile becoming icy; Ms Walsh is grand most of the time but you do not want to cross her.

'Grace?' says Ms Walsh. 'Any ideas?'

'Why do I think you think it's important, Miss?'

Ms Walsh makes the *uh-huh* sound.

'Because it's about abortion,' says Grace.

Ms Walsh makes the *go on* gesture.

'And that's an important issue,' says Grace.

'But why?' says Ms Walsh, and strides to the back of the room, waggling a pen and looking at no one in particular, and Grace is relieved to be absolved of the question, because Grace is not at all confident in her opinions, Grace is never sure exactly where they come from, whether they're just whispers from tweets and TV shows rolled into unsound judgement.

Momentarily she is upset when Ms Walsh chooses Samira to continue, because Samira is on the debating team, and so has an unfair advantage in English class. But then Molly writes 'SamirA, not SamirB' on her notebook for Grace to snigger at, and Grace does. Whatever, at least Grace and Molly know how to laugh.

Samira tells Ms Walsh that the issue is important, because abortion is illegal in Ireland, which is why the characters in the story had to be so secretive. Samira hopes then that Ms Walsh won't ask her for a more personal reaction, because she is not sure what she should say. This is a weird feeling, because Samira is proud of how articulate she is, how solid her viewpoints, how well thought-out her arguments. Samira hates being wrong and that is why she so rarely is wrong; she is anxious enough to check and double-check before putting forward facts. But this one is an opinion and there is no solid basis for an opinion in a context-less place; there are no statistics and few verified stories, because the issue is simply not meant to exist in Ireland; it is, therefore, stuck in the realm of fiction, short stories written by girls like Gráinne or poems written by activists.

Samira thinks, *I feel like the ban is wrong but I don't know that it's wrong,* and also she feels like if she offered her opinion, some of the girls would sneer and ask her what her parents would say to that? It is well known that Samira is not allowed to go out with boys.

'Wonderful!' cries Ms Walsh, as if the illegality of abortion is wonderful, thinks Shauna, which it certainly isn't.

'Come on, girls, be brave,' says Ms Walsh, 'A hearty fair play to whoever wants to kick off our discussion' and so, *Fine*, Shauna thinks, it falls to her to have the backbone yet again.

'We're the only country in Europe where abortion is illegal in nearly every case,' Shauna says. 'I saw a map online and it was mortifying.'

'What about the Vatican?' says Chinara.

'That's hardly a country,' Shauna says.

Shauna and Chinara aren't fond of one another, because Chinara is so loud, when Shauna – though she doesn't really know this of herself – thinks she should be the only loud one in the class, because she's genuinely passionate about things, whereas Chinara's just a clown.

Shauna's mother is a vet. She has only one sibling. She spends a lot of time with adults, both IRL and online, and sometimes school is a real pain in the hoop, because she has no interest at all in chart music or GAA[4] or going to discos, and she thinks that the girls who do are a little bit simple and certainly uninteresting. Though she did approve when Chinara dyed her hair ruby red. She told her mother and sister that Chinara's hair looked incredibly bold. She did not tell Chinara.

'The map was mortifying,' Shauna goes on. 'I think Ireland should bring its healthcare up to the European standard, because this is like, third-world shit. Sorry, Miss,' she says, as Ms Walsh purses her lips.

Maja is speaking even as her hand stretches over her head.

---

4   Gaelic Athletic Association

'Miss, I think it's not very constructive to drag on other countries if Ireland's no better. Like, when you say things like "third world" you just make people cross and then they go against you.'

'You're not from here, though,' Laura B says.

'So?' says Maja.

'So,' Laura B says, by way of a devastating burn; she sucks her teeth and leans back.

'Didn't Polish women riot for their right to abortion?' Shauna says.

'No, they protested,' Maja says.

'And that was for more than we have,' Shauna says.

'I'm not anti-abortion,' Maja says, 'but if I was, you wouldn't be making me pro, the way you're talking. That's all.'

'Do you think a more appropriate term is pro-choice?' Ms Walsh says, once again tilting her chin back so that she is addressing the whole room, and there is silence for a moment as the swell looks for somewhere to break, and so then Molly says, 'Yeah, but not completely.'

Ms Walsh circles the wrist of the hand that holds the biro.

'Like doesn't that mean you could change your mind at any point?' Molly says. 'What about the baby?'

Shauna tuts. 'Jesus, Molly, it's not a baby.'

'When did you become God?' Molly says.

'God should be kept out of the whole argument,' Shauna says.

'But if you're super religious then God is, like...' Maja widens her eyes. 'In every argument.'

'Well, he shouldn't be,' Shauna says, ''cos most of us are not super religious.'

'Yeah, human rights can't be decided by religious beliefs,' says Samira. 'Because not everyone has the same religion, but everyone has the same human rights.'

'Where's the baby's rights, though?' says Molly.

'How can you have rights if you haven't even been born yet?' Shauna says.

'Well, you should,' Molly says.

'Yeah, OK, and pay taxes too, so,' says Shauna.

'This is what I'm saying,' Maja says. 'Like how can you convince Molly if you're being mean to her?'

'I can do without her, that's how.'

'See, that's the kind of thing that makes people pro-life,' says Maja, triumphantly.

'I don't think so,' Samira says. 'People can't change their minds because the message is tough.'

'We shouldn't care if they do,' Shauna says.

'Then you're locking people out, and everyone's point of view is important,' Aifric says, and Jade says, 'Yeah, otherwise you're just as bad.'

'Just as bad as what?' Emily says.

'As them,' Jade says. 'People who push their views on everyone else.'

'Like Shauna,' Chinara says, and Maja laughs and Shauna scowls.

'Keep making stupid comments, Chinara,' Shauna says. 'Don't bother to get involved or anything.'

'Oh, did you ask me my opinion? No, you did not. Just speaking for everyone, like always. And really, what have you to complain about?'

'Not having healthcare? The same thing you have to complain about?'

'Don't tell me it's the same,' Chinara says. 'You don't know my life.'

'Chinara raises a good point,' Ms Walsh says. 'How do we include everyone in the conversation? Everyone's views are important if we want to have a healthy dialogue.'

'It's not the view, Miss, it's where the view comes from,' Chinara says. 'Shauna's rich, so she can't speak for me.'

'I didn't say I was speaking for you.'

'You said we have the same complaint.'

'We do – who cares where it comes from?'

'Yeah, Shauna's rich so what would she know?' Grace says, reviving this point with some glee.

Shauna makes a dismissive gesture. 'Oh my God,' she says, 'that's so stupid.'

'Miss, if Shauna's going on the pro side then I'm going on the anti side because calling people stupid is just not on,' says Maja.

'Are we doing an actual debate?' Samira asks.

'Look how excited Samira is now,' Jade says. 'Samira loves the debates, like.'

'Would you like to tackle this as a debate?' Ms Walsh asks.

'I'm game,' Shauna says, and Chinara pretends to faint.

'I take anti, I take anti!' Maja shouts.

'OK then, teams of three,' Ms Walsh says, and adds quickly, sternly, 'I'll choose the teams.'

'Can we do it properly?' Aifric says. 'As in, with rules, so no one shouts anyone down? Because I think the arguments will be kind of passionate otherwise and it's just easier if we're all respectful.'

'Of course,' Ms Walsh says. 'Of course. It's integral to debate, as most of you are aware.'

'Whatever,' Shauna says. 'Someone has to win.'

'Case in point,' Jade sighs.

'It's not always about winning, Shauna,' Ms Walsh says.

The girls take pens and paper and move about as Ms Walsh directs them. Maja and Shauna square up to one another, then smirk and high-five, each appreciative of the worthy opponent in the other. Aifric and Jade are pleased to find themselves on the same team, a sentiment that does not go unnoticed by Molly and Grace, who have been separated and who mutter darkly to one another about Ms Walsh playing favourites before they stomp off to join their groups. Chinara and Laura B are on a team with Samira, to Samira's horror and their great relief; both sit back and shrug and sigh as Samira grudgingly, helplessly starts working on notes. Emily catches Laura B's eye and gestures at Samira's bowed head and leers; Laura B guffaws.

'Which side would you like, Gráinne?' Ms Walsh generously asks. 'As you are the founder of this opportunity, as it were.'

'I don't know,' Gráinne says. 'I just wrote the story, like.'

'I'm guessing pro,' Ms Walsh says. 'Join Aifric and Jade,' and so Gráinne does, and looks sullen – many of the girls notice and put this down to Gráinne's sullen nature – although Gráinne is not actually sullen, at least not on this occasion; she is a little bit sick; she doesn't understand why this is a debate all of a sudden; her story is what it is, she thinks, where's the debate in that? The girls move desks and shuffle chairs, borrow paper, engage boisterously, design fancy bullet points. Gráinne leans back in her chair and Aifric charitably says, 'I told you it was a good story'.

'It's become a whole conversation,' says Jade.

Gráinne just says, 'Yeah.'

And cannot look at the points Aifric and Jade so carefully jot down.

Lisa McInerney is an award-winning novelist. Her books include *The Glorious Heresies* and *The Blood Miracles*.

15

ON NORTHERN IRELAND
SIOBHÁN FENTON

As we stand on the cusp of a referendum on the Eighth Amendment, there can be little doubt about it – the Republic of Ireland is experiencing a reproductive rights revolution. However, for Northern Irish campaigners, the moment is a bittersweet one.

The Repeal movement has long been plagued by a Northern Irish blind spot within the campaign. Northern Ireland is largely frozen out of the narrative surrounding what repealing the Eighth will mean and knowledge about reproductive rights in the northern corner of the island can be at times shockingly non-existent among Repeal campaigners.

As a writer and campaigner on Northern Ireland's abortion ban, I have been at times dumbfounded by the lack of awareness and interest that campaigners within the Repeal movement have shown about the nightmarish laws their northern neighbours are subjected to, just across the border. However, I have also been surprised and touched by the solidarity and warmth with which Repeal campaigners have embraced Northern Irish issues once they do have a grasp of the issues.

This chapter, therefore, seeks to explore the main issues involved in the Repeal movement's relationship with Northern

Ireland so far, as well as exploring the main opportunities for better awareness, support and solidarity. In this spirit, both campaigns have much to learn from and through each other for the better advancement of reproductive rights both in Northern Ireland and the Republic.

What I say here is based primarily on my experiences as an activist within the London-Irish Abortion Rights Campaign, where I sit on the Northern Irish committee, as well as my experiences as a Northern Irish journalist reporting on the ban and how it impacts on women's lives. There is, of course, no one way nor one right way to engage in activism. Rather, this chapter seeks to highlight some of the existing potential pitfalls and opportunities for positive change.

As the referendum approaches, it is important that the Northern Irish blind spot is looked squarely in the eye and addressed. To do so will be of benefit to campaigns for reproductive rights across the island.

How Northern Ireland came to be sidelined by Repeal
Despite being the Republic of Ireland's closest neighbour and having almost identically harsh abortion laws, Northern Ireland is seldom acknowledged by most within the Repeal movement.

This lack of engagement tends to stem from one of three key factors.

Firstly, there is little awareness of Northern Irish news, culture, politics or society, which is a natural consequence of Northern Ireland being a separate entity with a separate parliament and media from the Republic. Many within the Repeal movement simply do not know what Northern Ireland's abortion laws are, as they are not discussed in the Dáil or on RTÉ in the same way as the Republic's are.

Secondly, as Northern Ireland has a separate legal

jurisdiction from the Republic of Ireland, many in the Repeal movement wrongly assume that we have no stake in the reform, as people living in Northern Ireland are not bound by the Irish constitution.

This is an understandable misconstruction, and yet could not be further from the truth. Although Northern Ireland is not directly bound to follow the Irish constitution, its presence impacts on our lives and our access to reproductive rights. Sadly, we are far further behind the Republic in terms of public opinion and political will for reforming our own abortion ban. Repealing the Eighth Amendment, therefore, is the best opportunity for Northern Irish women to improve our access to abortion within the near future. If women can travel from Northern Ireland to the Republic for terminations, this would be a considerably less arduous and expensive option than travelling across to Great Britain. Last-minute flights and a hotel stay can cost hundreds of pounds, whereas a return bus ticket from Belfast is a mere £16, or a return train ticket costs £45. This price difference could make all the difference for low-income women. Similarly, passengers flying to Great Britain are often required to show a passport or other identification documents, which can prove prohibitive for undocumented women or those in abusive relationships. No such documentation is required to cross the Irish border. As Brexit looms, it is possible that this could change as the border hardens, but the British, Irish and EU delegations have all expressed their desire to see as little change to the border as possible.

Of course, Northern Irish women travelling to the Republic for abortions would be no substitute for us having reproductive rights in our own country. However, it would be a massive improvement upon the present nightmarish situation. Northern Irish women may not live under the direct jurisdiction of the Eighth Amendment, but its repeal would increase our options immensely.

The third and final obstacle to people within the Repeal movement engaging with Northern Ireland is fear of getting involved in the awkward and messy politics for which we are renowned. Northern Ireland is a post-conflict society, which has only recently emerged from the decades-old Troubles conflict about the constitutional status of the region. Many in the Repeal movement are understandably nervous about becoming involved in what they consider to be dark and dangerous politics, as they fear putting their foot in it due to being unaware of the many nuanced sensitivities of Northern Ireland.

Northern Ireland's abortion laws

In Northern Ireland, there is no constitutional ban on abortion like the Eighth Amendment in the Republic of Ireland's constitution. Instead, the laws that apply are a tangle of legislation strewn across the annals of history from the 1800s to the mid 1900s.

The primary legislation that regulates abortion in Northern Ireland is the 1861 Offences Against the Person Act. Written before women had the right to vote or the light bulb had been invented, this 150-year-old legislation makes abortion a criminal offence carrying a life sentence. The Act states:

> *Every woman, being with child, who, with intent to procure her own miscarriage, shall unlawfully administer to herself any poison or other noxious thing, or shall unlawfully use any instrument or other means whatsoever with the like intent, and whosoever, with intent to procure the miscarriage of any woman [is] to be kept in penal servitude for life.*

In 1937, a doctor was put on trial for performing an abortion on a teenage rape victim. Following the case, a judge held that terminations are permissible where: 'If the doctor is of the opinion, on reasonable grounds and with adequate knowledge, that the probable consequences of the continuance of the pregnancy will be to make the woman a physical or mental wreck.'

The term 'wreck' is not one typical of medical or legal terminology, resulting in much confusion and ambiguity about exactly how threatened a woman's health must be before she qualifies for a legal termination. It has been suggested by some practitioners that this term could be flexible enough in Northern Ireland to allow for terminations when a woman's mental or physical health could be seriously harmed. However, women have been understandably reluctant to act as test cases to challenge the laws, and so this ambiguity has remained.

In 1967, as social attitudes relaxed in Great Britain and the reproductive rights movement surged, the Abortion Act was introduced and effectively legalised abortion in Great Britain. However, the final sentence of the Act states that the Act 'does not extend to Northern Ireland'.

To this day, Northern Irish abortion law is primarily regulated by the 1861 Offences Against the Person Act and the 1937 case law.

Throughout the years, attempts have been made to reform the law and bring Northern Ireland into line with the rest of the UK. As the violence of the Troubles escalated, the Stormont parliament was suspended in 1972 and Northern Ireland was instead ruled directly from London. Direct rule was seen by some as an opportunity for progressive reform, but English governments have primarily shied away from making any such moves for fear of provoking backlash among the Northern Irish political parties.

In 2008, legislation that could have legalised abortion in Northern Ireland was put to Westminster. However, it was purportedly blocked by the Labour MP and then Home Secretary Harriet Harman in exchange for the DUP (which is vehemently anti-choice) supporting then Prime Minister Tony Blair's controversial policy of forty-two-day detention without trial for terror suspects. For many pro-choice activists in Northern Ireland, this has been an insult for which they have never fully forgiven the Labour Party. While Harriet Harman is considered by many women in England as a feminist icon due to her work to advance gender equality during her time in office in other regards, for many in Northern Ireland she will always be the woman who sold her Northern Irish sisters down the river.

Since this debacle, as power-sharing at Stormont has seen devolution established in Northern Ireland, MPs at Westminster largely agree that only Stormont can change the abortion laws and that it would be both inappropriate and potentially a violation of constitutional law for them to do so.

For many pro-choice people living in Northern Ireland, the situation can be an extremely frustrating one. Simply put, few in Great Britain realise what Northern Ireland's abortion laws are and fewer still speak out about the injustice. The silence can at times feel deafening.

It is often reported in the media that abortion is legal in the UK, with Northern Ireland being entirely forgotten about. Elsewhere, women's magazines or political journals on abortion laws will focus on the UK as a whole, with a few sentences from a quick Google search about Northern Ireland tacked on the end as an apologetic afterthought.

On occasions when the laws are discussed, it is in the context that devolution must be respected and that the UK has no right to involve itself in Stormont's legal right to ban abortion. The prevailing discourse is that the situation in Northern Ireland is regrettable, but that it has little to do with people in Great Britain, who see themselves as having no legal or moral responsibility on the matter.

In November 2015, the Belfast High Court ruled that Northern Ireland's abortion laws constitute a breach of European human rights law in criminalising women who terminate following rape, incest or fatal foetal abnormality. In 2016, a vote was held at Stormont on whether to legalise abortion in these circumstances; however, it failed to pass. The 2015 ruling was appealed by the Attorney General on behalf of the Northern Irish government, and in June 2017 the Court of Appeals refused to uphold the Belfast High Court judgement. The Court of Appeals found that it was not appropriate for the courts to rule on abortion laws and that only Stormont could decide whether to instigate reform. This case is now expected to be appealed again to the Supreme Court.

Arrests of and police raids on Northern Irish women
Unlike the Republic of Ireland, where it is unheard of in modern times for police to intervene and arrest women for having abortions, women in Northern Ireland are often subject to police action and legal proceedings. This has increased in recent years, with the number of women being arrested on suspicion of committing abortions steadily climbing. It is hard to know precisely why the numbers are rising, but it is thought to be due in part to an increased number of women buying abortion pills online and having them sent to Northern Ireland, rather than travelling to Great Britain for terminations in clinics.

In April 2016, a deeply disturbing case highlighted the cruelty of Northern Ireland's abortion ban. The Belfast High Court heard the case of a twenty-one-year-old woman who had performed an abortion on herself. The court was told that the woman, then aged nineteen, had experienced a crisis pregnancy. She desperately tried to raise enough money to travel to Great Britain in time but had been unable to. In desperation, she ordered pills online and performed an abortion on herself at home in Northern Ireland. Her flatmates found out when they discovered foetal remains and bloodstained clothes in their kitchen bin. They then reported her to the police, who arrested her. The young woman was found guilty in the High Court and given a suspended sentence.

At the time of writing, another woman is due to stand trial. She is accused of helping her then fifteen-year-old daughter have an abortion. It is alleged that the girl was in an abusive relationship and felt she was too young to become a mother. Her mother allegedly helped her get abortion pills in Northern Ireland and disclosed this to her GP, who subsequently informed police.

On International Women's Day in 2017, while feminist activists were marching in a pro-choice parade, the police also raided the homes of a well-known local feminist campaigner, looking for abortion pills, sparking fears among pro-choice people of a clampdown.

Likelihood of reforming the abortion ban in Northern Ireland
There is little political appetite for reform, despite public support. Northern Ireland is subject to a similar gap in attitudes to the Republic of Ireland, whereby majority opinion in favour of reform is not matched by the attitudes of elected politicians. A 2016 poll by Amnesty International found that 72 per cent of people support abortion access for women who have conceived as a result of rape or incest, as well as 67 per cent support for instances of fatal foetal abnormality.

Northern Ireland's unique political circumstances also hamper any chance of reforming the abortion ban. The constitutional question of whether Northern Ireland should remain in the UK or reunite with the Republic of Ireland remains the gravitational centre around which all other political issues revolve. Politics remain divided on so called 'orange' (Protestant/Unionist/Loyalist) and 'green' (Catholic/Nationalist/Republican) lines.

Northern Ireland's largest party, the Democratic Unionist Party, is a right-wing, socially conservative Christian party and is vehemently opposed to any reform of abortion law. The smaller, more moderate Unionist party, the Ulster Unionists, has no official stance, instead designating it a matter of personal conscience for members; many are vocally anti-choice and few support reform.

The largest nationalist party, Sinn Féin, holds a slippery and malleable position on abortion. As a self-described socialist party, its members are split into those who support reform on grounds of social justice, and others who are conscious that many of their voters identify as Roman Catholics, so would not support a pro-choice party. Perhaps as a result, Sinn Féin supports limited reform in an attempt to keep both competing factions on side, which would be decriminalisation of abortion solely in instances of rape, incest or fatal foetal abnormality. The smaller, more moderate nationalist party, the Social Democratic and Labour Party, is completely opposed to abortion in all circumstances.

Among middle-ground parties, some support for reform has emerged. The centre political party, Alliance, considers it a matter of personal conscience for their politicians. A number of its high-profile politicians, Anna Lo and Naomi Long, have been passionate and outspoken in advocating the pro-choice position. Similarly, the Green Party remains small, with just two seats at Stormont. The party is pro choice, and one of its elected politicians and party Deputy Leader, Clare Bailey, has been a staunch ally of the pro-choice cause.

For the most part, Northern Ireland's abortion ban is not considered a pressing political issue. Every day radios and TV screens throughout Northern Ireland beam out news bulletins still primarily dominated by decades-old debates about where loyalist marching bands can parade, what role the Irish language should play and whether Protestant and Catholic children should attend the same schools. In the bluntest terms, the abortion ban is not an issue on the political agenda, which continues to centre on Northern Ireland's 'orange v. green' politics. The abortion laws receive scant coverage in the press and are scarcely ever mentioned on the doorstep at election time.

The Northern Irish pro-choice movement has not succeeded in obtaining the same critical momentum as the Repeal movement in the Republic, so far. We are much further behind in our fight for reform.

Campaigns for reform

The main campaign group in Northern Ireland fighting for reform is Alliance For Choice, which has been leading calls for change for over two decades. Based both in Belfast and Derry/Londonderry, the group campaigns for full decriminalisation of abortion through lobbying, organising protests and marches, coordinating information sessions and liaising with local and international press to highlight the reality of the laws.

Amnesty International also campaigns on the issue, as well as the Northern Ireland Human Rights Commission.

In 2016, the London-Irish Abortion Rights Campaign was established to campaign for free, safe and legal abortion throughout the island of Ireland. The Northern Ireland committee, of which I am a member, campaigns on the issue, including liaising with London-based MPs, journalists and lawyers to highlight the ban in Northern Ireland and campaign for change.

The DUP–Conservative pact and Northern Irish women's rights as a proxy war

Great Britain's lack of interest in Northern Ireland's abortion ban suddenly changed in the immediate aftermath of the June 2017 general election result. After news broke that the Conservatives had failed to reach a majority and would instead need to enter into a pact with the DUP to command a majority in parliament, online search queries about the DUP spiked. Now faced with the prospect of having the DUP at the heart of the national government, English feminists and the English left suddenly had a change of heart. As one Conservative MP speculated on BBC Radio 4 that the DUP might try to reduce term limits for abortions in England, Scotland and Wales, the feminist movement, which had marginalised and ignored Northern Irish women for generations, suddenly mobilised.

Marches against the DUP were held outside Parliament in Westminster, column inches were suddenly crammed with outrage about the DUP's backward policies and MPs clambered over each other to denounce them. At home in Northern Ireland, pro-choice activists watched with bemusement as England suddenly woke up to a mere glimpse of what has been our lived reality for decades. While the sudden solidarity was welcome, it was difficult not to feel bitterness at the essential message from England; it was OK when they did it to Northern Irish women, but if they think they can restrict the reproductive rights of women who actually matter, they should expect a revolution.

It became clear to left-wing politicians that the easiest way to undermine the Conservatives during their pact with the DUP was by attacking the Democratic Unionists and highlighting the policies which were most likely to cause embarrassment for the Conservatives. This was evidenced when one of Labour's main attack lines during the Queen's Speech under the Conservative–DUP government was to add an amendment calling on NHS England to give free abortions to women who travel from Northern Ireland, overturning a discriminatory policy whereby Northern Irish women have been forced to pay for terminations privately when they travel to England, despite being UK taxpayers. It was an issue that both Alliance For Choice in Northern Ireland and the London-Irish Abortion Rights Campaign in Great Britain had been highlighting for years, but which had fallen on deaf ears. Now, however, a sufficient number of Labour MPs were willing to back it in order to embarrass the Conservatives over their DUP partnership. The Conservatives finally cracked and agreed they would set up a system to fund abortions in Great Britain for Northern Irish women who have travelled over.

This was a great victory and a much-needed policy change, which will help middle- and lower-middle-class women, who will no longer have to pay hundreds of pounds for a termination in England. However, it did little to address the fact that low-income women will still struggle to find the funds to travel to England at short notice, that undocumented women will not have the required passport to make the trip, that women in abusive relationships may not be able to escape their partner's watch in order to go, or that women with disabilities may not be able to take the arduous journey. Although the policy was a step in the right direction, it did little to help some of the most vulnerable women in Northern Irish society or address the fundamental injustice in expecting women to leave their home region to access healthcare. There continues to be scant interest in legalising abortion in Northern Ireland through Westminster, or sincere engagement with Northern Irish politicians to encourage them to legalise it themselves at Stormont.

Therefore, while the policy change to give Northern Irish women free abortions in Great Britain was welcome, the progress was bittersweet for many Northern Irish pro-choice activists. We had secured the change we wanted but only while being positioned as a prop for the English left, to be wielded when useful for their causes but without any sincere engagement in the issues we face. Northern Irish women's wombs were now the battle site for a proxy war between the Labour party and the Conservatives in England.

Northern Ireland and the Repeal campaign as we approach the referendum

The reality is that the Republic of Ireland will most likely have access to free, safe and legal abortion long before women in Northern Ireland will. As it stands, we are decades, if not generations off seeing Stormont reach a position whereby it will legalise abortion through a parliamentary vote.

For us, therefore, our most realistic hope for imminent change lies in the surrounding jurisdictions. In relation to Great Britain, this has meant feminists there showing more solidarity – following the Conservative government giving Northern Irish women free abortions in England – and continuing to put pressure on Westminster to denounce Northern Ireland's laws, particularly in condemning the recent arrests and prosecutions. In the Republic of Ireland, our greatest hope comes in abortion access being increased there.

If Northern Irish women are able to travel to the Republic of Ireland to access abortion, that would be a vast improvement on being forced to travel by boat or by plane to Great Britain. This would be no substitute for reform of our own abortion laws, but for the most marginalised women in Northern Ireland, it would constitute a major improvement.

Unfortunately, there has been little discussion or consideration so far by the Repeal movement as to the practicalities involved in Northern Irish women travelling to the Republic for abortions in the event of a successful Repeal referendum. For instance, it is unknown if Northern Irish women could be required to pay for abortions in the Republic of Ireland, or would be entitled to a reimbursement from the NHS.

As it stands, people from Northern Ireland who are in the Republic of Ireland at the time of needing an operation do not have to pay, unlike locals. Following medical treatment, those with Northern Irish addresses are sent an invoice by the hospital and have to respond with their NHS number in order for the NHS to reimburse the hospital of all the costs. It is unknown if the same reimbursement would apply to abortions, or if Northern Irish women would have to pay.

Furthermore, the Northern Irish activists' role in the referendum campaign has yet to be explored. There is much enthusiasm in Northern Ireland among pro-choice people to actively participate in the Repeal referendum campaign, whether by travelling down to the Republic to knock on doors, participating in social media campaigns, fundraising for Repeal, or attending rallies and protests in the Republic. However, many feel unsure about whether our involvement would be welcome from Repeal campaigners, who may not consider this to be truly 'our battle' too. In addition, some anxiety exists as to whether our presence at Repeal events or campaign sessions could undermine the movement, as some of those canvassed may consider us to be 'blow-ins' with no clear connection to the

Repeal cause and thereby rendering the Repeal campaign less authentic in the eyes of some voters.

There is a wealth of enthusiasm and solidarity to tap into among Northern Irish pro-choice activists, which can enrich the Repeal movement by adding extra resources and talent to the referendum campaign.

Similarly, the Repeal campaign could do much to return this solidarity by attending rallies and protests in Northern Ireland, lobbying TDs[5] to speak out about the injustice of ongoing arrests and prosecutions, as well as meeting with Northern Irish campaigners to share thoughts, experiences and resources.

Although women in Northern Ireland and the Republic of Ireland are not subject to the exact same laws on abortion, we are sadly subjected to the same human rights abuses and denial of both dignity and basic healthcare. For this reason, solidarity is essential for the reproductive-rights movements throughout the island to reach their full potential. The pending Repeal referendum is a vital opportunity to finally look the Northern Irish blind spot squarely in the eye.

Siobhán Fenton is a Northern Irish journalist who reports on gender and politics for the *New Statesman*, the *Spectator*, the BBC and the *Independent*. She has reported on Northern Ireland's abortion laws for many years. She is a member of the Northern Irish committee in the London-Irish Abortion Rights Campaign.

---

[5] Members of the Irish parliament, Teachta Dála

16

HEARTBREAK

EMMET KIRWAN

Heartbreak.
Young one wakes
to the morning after.
Sees graffiti marker
Her friend's names written on the rafter
Of her sister's bunk, who's no longer there.
Disappeared.
A feather blown to the night winds where someday young one
hopes to follow.
Black permanent smell, sweet and spells,
Christine
1916
Deborah
Up The RA
Jenny loves Carl
Taylor is a slag
I love Sean.

Her face is a picture of grace
As she reaches, touches, runs her hand along the bunk.
Thump thump thump
Now whodathunk
Her ma made it home.
She'll be early morning lucid
When Mam's hazy
She lets young one and friends sit in the box room
Listen to tunes
Smoke squidgy like cave mens
From the BC whens
They wrote the happy story of their lives on the bedroom wall
It belies a hurt narrative.

The ma, fuck does not give
Cos she's wellouvih
The daddy, the picture, well he has been ouhvih
Recently young one has got breasts and attention
And not just boys, I should mention
But fully grown men who remark
'She's an old 15, but an absolute 10'
And that was when the boys started yelling,
'Here, here, here, c'mere, c'mere, c'mere,
Let me shout sweet obscenities in your ear.'

Heartbreak

She does double take
and sees Sean
She feels she likes this one boy because he didn't shout
No

Young one is special, young fella said
She always thought her first time would be in a bed.
Not a wet patch of grass with a dog barking at the back end of
where two housing estates meet.
And I think when he said it, he meant it
He truly did.
Because he's not like all the other boys, but he is still just a boy
who's pulling out late and now pulling out early.
She sits in a chemist queue
for a patronising talking-to
'Well if I knew it was gonna happen I wouldn't be here talking
to you.'
So she bounces.
Weeks later, stomach follows suit.
Sister, no longer there for a voice, if they were together they
could be stronger
And one of her friends simply said, 'Stinger.'

Her ma said, 'Here, c'mere, c'mere, c'mere
Look listen, understand there's no money for a trip on the ringer,
that's only for those that can.'

Heartbreak

But now she's wide awake
No longer dropping yokes, but dropping little prenatal vit hit
No longer smoking rollies with a little nodge of squidgy
She thinks, this little nodge in me that I see from this strangely
rendered orange 3D picture of my little
Squidgy.

It doesn't look or feel real
And the chemicals that at 12 started running riot and are only now after settling down
are whipped up into a frenzy
Sensation of emotion puts her head on a brink and she thinks

Heartbreak

She had the baby on her own
but for its sake, she resolves to love this thing more that she was ever loved herself
But the gaff is still ill
The owl one's on the thrill and the back ends and the hallways are still full of new
'C'mere, c'mere's'
Every weekend

So she kicks it
To a back alley B&B
Asks a grubby blueshirted TD for help and the problem compounds when he says
'Go back to your mam's'
Sound

Newspaper learns of her predicament.
Asks for a photography and an interview
So she rocks this little €15 boo hoo
Made by her counterpart on the other side of the globe

'Look at her, she looks fine to me.
My tax euros means she gets everything for free.'

'What about cherishing all of the children equally?'
'Was a poet's way of describing Catholics and Protestants living harmoniously under one flag
Not so my taxes could pay for a house for a working-class slag.'

Heartbreak

But now it's money she'll have to make.
Young one grows and gets a job just to prove them all wrong
She kicks the rhyme in a zero-hour contract
No overtime
How can you work your way out of poverty
And down, down, down, down downtrodden property
And keep getting poorer while working she shouts
because prices go up and wages go down
Now she'll have to do more
To change this salacious situation
Progression she feels will only come through education.

The boy grows tall and strong and school becomes a place for the two
Now inspired by her brilliant teacher she's got that yearnin' for learnin'
But she's not learnin' for earnin', no she's just learnin' for learnin's sake
So she can articulate
this incandescent rage between all the young women of Ireland in 2016
She learns things, like constitutional refusal of bodily autonomy
Thinks this is backwards blasphemy

You mean, as a woman or plebeen in this country of opportunity
This ceiling and seas are shamrock-coloured green glass to me
You'll only get the last of me
And still dealing with the ignominy
Of getting followed and hollered at in the street in spite of undergraduate accomplishment
'Relax darling, take it as a compliment.'
Boys, leave it out, look at her
She's a mother

She says, 'Stop! Here! C'mere, c'mere, c'mere
I am not defined by the fact that I am some man's daughter, sister, cousin, mother.
I am a woman. And I have agency just because I'm breathing air, motherfucker
and I'm standing here, motherfucker.
And you, and this State are the ones who are trying to fuck me.'

The boy sees this treatment in the street and from the State all his life
He decides to regulate.
But young one now, fully grown, tries to sate this rage and build a young man
This young boy. He will be the best elements of femininity wrapped in a rebellious feminine but benign masculinity.
The man she always hoped for.
He will love you 'til the end of days
Traverse space and time and do even more
And with her words, her life, a mixture of loving and ethics, food in his belly and all the right seasoning
From the instant he achieves cognitive reasoning and a maturity he will be the man to settle up the score

and say, 'Here, ma, you embody all that is good and are the one that I am fighting for. I'll never catcall. I'll treat and respect and help create an Ireland that will stand in awe of all mná.'

Heartbreak

Heart mend.

Emmet Kirwan is an award-winning playwright, poet and actor.

17

TO BE INCLUDED AND HEARD
ELLIE KISYOMBE

It was Friday morning and I remember I was lying on my bed after a long, tiring day. I heard this soft voice and the lady asked me, 'Am I speaking to Ellie?' I said, 'Yes.' She said, 'I want to invite you to come and speak on the march.' I said, 'What march?' Since my life is full of protest, I didn't understand exactly. I thought it was about another End Direct Provision[6] march, and since that's what I do, I said, 'Yes!'

I said I was in Cork now, and they said it didn't matter, they'd find a way for me to make it there. I asked what the theme of the event was. The lady replied, 'It's about Repeal the Eighth.'

Then my head started pounding. I started getting rage, and at the same time I was so scared I wasn't sure what I am going to say.

But in my heart I had too much to spit out! I started thinking about the fact that I am on the brink of fighting my status. Not only that, even the Thirteenth Amendment ['this subsection shall not limit freedom to travel between the State and another

---

6   Direct Provision is the system the Republic of Ireland uses for asylum seekers until their application has been dealt with, housing many for years.

state'] does not represent me. Is this really something I want to get involved in and start crying about? I battled my heart out. Inside me, there was a huge conflict between my heart and my instinct. But my instinct kept telling me: 'You are right, you need to do this.'

I started thinking of migrant women who have died in a way seeking abortion, and some nearly committing suicide. The thought of Savita [Halappanavar] would not leave me. I know I didn't know her, but as a migrant and an asylum-seeker woman, I thought, despite us not meeting or being friends – even coming from different continents – we were aligned in Ireland and faced the same marginalisation. That gave me courage to believe I needed to do this.

I thought of Miss A, who went into a total depression and became suicidal because she was not allowed to get an abortion. I said to myself: 'I have to do this. It doesn't matter whether I am just going to be a number or whether I am going to be heard or not, I will do this.'

On the other hand I started doubting myself, thinking I am a migrant and coming from a very strong Christian background, and these issues are not talked about a lot. There are a lot of judgements. How will my people look at me? I felt discomfort in me, but at the back of my mind I kept saying to myself, 'This is not right.' It has to be said, there are a lot of migrant women who are dying because of cultural beliefs they don't want to talk about, not because they choose not to speak, but they are scared to do so. This is not a matter I should simply think about, but a matter I should talk about. I don't need to be like my fellow migrant women who are silenced by cultural beliefs and fear; if I choose to be silent, I will silence everybody. But if I will go out and speak, do I even know how many women I will save? With that in my mind, I packed my bags.

Friday afternoon I left Cork. I got to Dublin late. I got home to see my kids. They asked me, 'Mum, are you back from school?' I said, 'No, I have an important event to go to tomorrow.' So all night I started writing my speech. I wrote the first one; I scrapped it; second, third. I wasn't sure, and then I said to myself, 'I am just going to go and show up and start ranting as I normally do!' In the morning, I left home for the Memorial Gardens in Dublin. I saw a huge group of men and women. I was so shocked. I didn't expect that, as most of the events I speak at I don't see that number of people.

I pinched myself. I said, 'Ellie, you can do it.' I was terrified. A friend of mine asked me if I was OK. I said, 'I am not sure, but I hope I will be.' She held my hand as we marched up to Merrion Square, and when I reached there, I was given a bottle of water. I was among ten women who came to the platform. The first lady spoke, and the second, and then it was my turn. I wasn't sure I could say anything, but then in my mind I started thinking of Savita and Miss A. Then I went into a rage, thinking of me as an asylum seeker and knowing that I don't have rights in a country where I believe there's so much democracy. Something just came inside of me and I started talking. I shouted. I shouted as if I was fighting myself. I started hearing from the audience – cheers, clapping hands. I said to myself, 'I did it!' I made it to Dublin and on behalf of migrant women I have spoken.

I started getting messages of congratulations. One said, 'Our sister, you're our hero.' I said to myself, 'I don't need to be your hero, but someone needed to get out there and do something different and I have just done that.' I felt so free, although I was not free, but I felt liberated. I saw myself in the news article and a friend of mine said to me, 'I have seen a lot of Repeal writings in newspapers, but not a lot of them mention asylum seekers or migrant women, but you just put all of us on the map.'

After that I didn't feel scared at all. I never thought of my cultural beliefs, my Christianity. The feeling inside me was so liberating, free. I heard from people who were there who were celebrities. I was like, well, who would have known that an asylum-seeking women will be in front of celebrities and Irish communities fighting for her inclusion and the need to change the way the government makes their policies regarding migrant women on abortion? I pray one day that all of us, we will be included and heard, and that it's our bodies, our choice, a human right.

Ellie Kisyombe is a Direct Provision activist, challenging the conditions asylum seekers are housed in in Ireland, and the co-founder of Our Table, a non-profit community and food organisation.

18

THREE: THREE
TARA FLYNN

three: one

Ireland slips over the horizon and I am in the middle of the sea, the Irish Sea. I am numb, but it is time to turn around. To face where I am going. The other side not yet visible. Beneath my feet, a hundred cars – a thousand? – I don't know. I can never tell. I'm not good with numbers. Beneath them again, one of the deepest, shortest stretches of water. In Europe? The world? I don't know. Though I was better at geography than maths. I need to find the loo. I might be sick. I should stay near one. I will need to pee more than once on this short trip.

The first time I left home, left Ireland behind, was on a ferry, just like this. A family holiday, car and all. I wanted to take the dog, but he stayed behind with neighbours. Instead, a school of dolphins jumped along beside and we tried to take a picture but too much flare means I am all that's visible, like an angel on the deck, though there are sparkles on the sea where dolphins had just been.

A school trip, years later. We all got on the bus, drove across the country, cassettes playing, singing, and then boarded the ship. We couldn't believe we were getting away with all going away together. We watched a movie none of us should yet have seen, but there was no one checking at the door of the ship's cinema. We all had nightmares afterwards. Some of the lads bought booze. In Stratford, we saw a play we were studying. Then we did it all in reverse.

And now I cross, alone. Just me and plastic seats fixed to the ground in a way I wish my feet were fixed to the soil so I could have stayed at home. I could have stayed at home without fear that my treacherous body might somehow float up into the air and away from where I am not wanted. I do not own my body any more and my country does not own me. Does not want to. I have been given up. Farmed out. My country doesn't afford me the backward glances I gave it as we pulled away from shore. I am cut adrift.

It's so sentimental, isn't it? To love the land and think it loves us back. Pride is demanded and isn't hard to give. But one wrong move... One wrong move and we are banished.

I buy a horrid coffee and it's horrid, but I don't have enough cash to change it for a watery tea and so I drink the horrid coffee. There's some strange comfort in the horridness of it. It has something about it of every horrid coffee gone before; it's not new or frightening and, for now, that will do.

A telly is on somewhere. I couldn't tell you what's on it. The luckier people sleep – I don't know how they manage it – on the plastic chairs or squished up on backpacks. Ninety minutes, the crossing. The sea is smooth and calm. I cannot contemplate what I would have done if we had not crossed today. If sailing were postponed. I have connections to make, as well as to sever. I must be on time.

I was late, you see. I don't know why I'm telling you this. Because you don't know me and I'll never see you again, maybe? At home, everyone knows everyone. Or if they don't, they assume. Fill in the blanks for who you probably are. Not rounded out, not fully a person, but someone who plays some kind of role in your life and will hopefully recede when that's been played.

I am a euphemism, now. I'm *going to England*. I was late and surprised that I was late. Shocked, even. I've been so careful. No spring chicken, isn't that what they say? Haha. *Haha*. But something didn't work and something biological did and here I am. I'm going to England and I hope I make my train.

I make my train. I want to sit away from anyone I sat near on the boat. The drivers have already gone below deck for their cars. The rest of us bolt on foot. The train's right there; we don't have to bolt far. I've been here before, on happier, easier journeys. *Sail & Rail*. To London for a few days. Or to Manchester for a cheap flight to somewhere hot. I know this ferry-port. No way I could forget it now.

I get a tea now (my 'train money') from the trolley. It settles my stomach, uneasy from the crossing and … you know. The day has dawned. The morning's moving on as surely as the carriage.

I have transferred the directions from the internet onto a piece of paper folded into my pocket and consulted many times. It takes me a while to find the place. I can't take a taxi – I do have 'taxi money', but that's for later. After. When I don't want to think; might not be able. And I will need someone else to guide me back the way I came.

I find the place. Not too many of 'them' outside, just one man with a gory picture. He doesn't insist. Probably only waking up himself, and the shield formed of my determination seems enough to put him off.

Inside. It's clean. Not too busy, but then, it's early yet. I am too early. Much. I gave myself plenty of time. I give my name. They check my name. And then the questions start and they are brisk but kind. More plastic chairs. I don't drink any more tea, don't know if I am allowed.

I don't read my book. I take out my book and look at it, but words won't go in. This is awful. I'm so glad that I am here.

three: two

I'm a great walker, I always was. I tell people that's why my skin is still so good; they think I'm in my thirties and almost have a fit when I tell them I'm fifty. Nothing like a nice, long walk to clear the head. I pop on a layer of the moisturiser from the blue tub – if it was good enough for my mother, then it's good enough for me! – and head out. I don't listen to music. I like to let the silence overtake me and He steers me in the direction I should go. All weathers. It's even nicer if it rains, to be honest. The raindrops sting my skin, making it pink and fresh.

With three almost-grown up kids still at home and a full life, time alone is a luxury; I often head off before they're all awake. Barry will get youngest's lunch done if I'm slightly later than usual. This is rare. I have it down to a fine art now. I leave when it's still dark most of the year, clicking the door as softly as I can so's not to disturb the gentle breaths upstairs. I'm filled with love at the thought of them. This isn't an escape; I see it more as a cleansing preparation for the day ahead.

By the time I'm on my way back, it's getting light. There are more cars, the smog is thickening and the streets no longer all my own. To make up for it, I've started to take a small detour to the new bakery. It's not cheap, but if you can't treat yourself...! They have hot cross buns there at the moment, oddly traditional among the cosmopolitan croissants and Danish pastries and cupcake pops. *A reminder. If you look for Him, He's there.* Even when you'd think He'd been forgotten. I usually get a scone, a muesli scone, which really makes it neither, but it tastes good and makes me feel healthy. Today I take one of the buns and smile. *I see You. I heard You speak to me.*

The chimney towers over the block the bakery's on and so I see it every day. I don't like to think about it; I'm sure He knows and guides me past if for this very reason. The Church did terrible things, once upon a time, in trying to do good. They put girls in there, in different times, different times, bad girls, girls with nowhere else to go. Girls beyond help, in many ways. Mam always reminded me how lucky I was to have the things I had and know the things I know. She taught me that though these girls had sinned, still they were taken in. The kindness of it. Now, I'm the first to say some clergy got it wrong. Of course they did. Of course. But they really did a lot of good. We mustn't forget that and tar them all with the same brush.

Freshly bagged bun in hand, I pass the red-brick chimney stack and notice something unfamiliar in the wire mesh of the building's gates. Flowers. Not wild, not dandelions threaded there by some passing toddler. These have been bought at the florist's on the corner (I know the wrapping; I use her a lot) and placed with care. A reaction to the recent revelations, I'm sure. I'm sure this was meant as a kindly gesture, but in their cellophane wrapping, they seem to me incongruously bright – disrespectful, almost. For some reason I cannot help or explain, anger burns my stomach.

People will look for any reason to denigrate the Church now. And those of us who fight for it, who fight to keep Ireland from losing any shred of morality it had, they try to silence us. They say we're outdated, cruel; *homophobes*, they say. *Misogynists*. I'm a woman myself. A feminist – aren't I raising two girls and a respectful young man? It is crazy what they'll say, especially when we fight for the unborn. Well, I'm not ashamed. But now they'll use these new revelations against us. Take old cruelties and lump us all together. They're the cruel ones, wanting to end inconvenient pregnancies. If only they realised what a gift they have been given.

My eldest was a surprise. But we knew what we had to do, and moved the wedding up. It wasn't easy – of course not! No one is saying it is! – but we wouldn't do any different if we'd the time again. We are blessed, lucky that He has given us wisdom enough to see it. I remember, I fell in love with Barry when I realised he was as passionate about his faith as I was about my own. You don't see too much of it now. But we lead by example wherever we can.

I don't judge these girls. Of course I don't. Sure amn't I human myself? I make mistakes! They don't know any better. Some of them aren't the brightest to begin with and then they get themselves into a vulnerable situation (if you know what I mean) with unsuitable men (if you know what I mean) and I'm sure it's very stressful. How could anyone cope with all that? Someone has to look out for them. If that has to be me, fine. We all have our vocation. This is what He wants me to do. *Thank You.*

I don't mean to smile; what we're discussing isn't funny. It's deathly serious, of course. I just sometimes feel overwhelmed with the burden of the duty I've accepted, honoured though I am to accept it. That brings some joy.

I hurry, head down, past the laundry. The wind rattles the cellophane and I can hear it still, even when I round the corner onto the main street and the home stretch. I pass my church and feel instantly better. The anger abates. Here is my home from home. It's where I find my tribe. Our collective past built into its solid walls; the laundry gates dwarfed, nothing at all compared. I will stand at the altar rails next Sunday, my family by my side, and dispense the Holy Eucharist from my own cleansed hands and heart.

Mea culpa. Mea culpa. Mea culpa.

three: three

If I had to look into her clear blue eyes, I'm not sure I'd be able. I'm working on it. For now, I do it from here. Telling her. Putting her in her place. A safe distance. Safe for her.

Whore. I'll write. *Slut.* Things I'd never say to her face, though I type them quick enough. I want to shock that bitch. You can't let them away with it, y'see. Once she's shocked, she might stop. Might think. Then she'll know who's right.

It's a fucking *rush.*

My favourite profile is the one where I'm a woman. Like *Catfish*, but the wrong way round – instead of getting them to believe I love them, I want them to feel my hate. I let it burn, pouring out my fingers 'til the poison becomes words. Toxic messages. Acid, maybe. Maybe it'll melt their screens! I know, when they react, it's melted their minds.

And her, not like the rest. She eats at me. Irritates. I don't know why she's got under my skin. I dream about her. In the dream, she burns, not me. I try to save her, but the flames are already round her and by the time it's too late, I understand that this is how it was supposed to end. I'm merely an observer. I agitate. That's what I do. I bring them to where they're supposed to be.

Some people see through the parts I play – I think she does. She called me by my real name that time and my heart thumped faster. It's not like she won; I'd never let her win. 'Cos I was not unmasked. But I felt good. Seen. If she picked up clues it's 'cos I left them for her, like crumbs in darkened woods.

She ignores me now, the stupid cunt. But I am going nowhere. I agitate and I will escalate.

They think they can protect her, but they can't. I can do this all day. They dogpile on me when she types words she thinks are caustic and gives them my scent, sends them out, but she is only bringing them to me. The fucking fools. I love it. I'm the one who tastes the blood.

They secretly respect me. They appreciate good banter. Sparring. They give me much more time than she. In real life, they'd buy me pints and we'd have a laugh, so we would. It's all healthy debate, at the end of the day.

Pushing past discomfort's how we learn. They need to learn. Punishment helps lessons stick. People need to take a long look at themselves. I'm the mirror.

The truth? I don't care. Not personally, not really. I don't care what sluts do, with who or where they do it, or whether they get pregnant or stay pregnant or not. Condoms? Me? Nah. Never liked the feel. And if some bitch lets things get that far, doesn't look out for herself, then why would I look out for her? I'm not her husband. Husband? Who'd marry a slut like her? She'll die alone, the libtard bitch. Haha.

Told you I didn't care. I don't care.

I don't like posting harsher stuff when Mam's downstairs. She'd never see it – she won't go online, I do all her emails – but I still don't like the feeling. She taught me right, my Mam. I know how to treat a lady. A decent one. One who deserves it. What the fuck happened to decency, ha? To traditional values? I'm not the one who's out of step. It's the world that's gone mad.

Girls I know, ones I went to school with, like, we made our communion and our confirmation together (oh, they don't like religion but they took the cash quick enough, didn't they?), they're not one bit afraid to say the most disgusting things now. To wear words on their chests that might as well say 'Murder' and it's getting out of hand. We will need strong hands to get things back to how they were. I'll be those hands. What's right is right.

Yer one. The shameless one. Her blue eyes clear, her blonde

hair straight. She looks like Mam. But she is not like Mam. Mam would never have killed me, *killed me, like*! in her womb and not looked back. I will tell you this now and – listen – hear me out. I don't know anyone like that.

And if I knew someone like that I would speak to them kindly and thank them. I would not mean it, but it would be the decent thing to do. Establish trust. Phase two is to remind her and anyone who's listening of what it is she has done. Make them see it. Show them. Shock them into sense. Remind her that she should be ashamed. That she should beg for forgiveness, do her penance on her knees and then, maybe then, we can love her again.

I want her voice to tremble. I want her hands to shake. I want her eyes to fill with tears and not be able to tear her gaze from mine when I see into her soul and she can't hide. She will not be defiant when we meet. She will crumble into dust.

And I will take her in my arms and tell her that she is forgiven. I will carry her to where she will be safe.

I will save her from herself, the filthy slut.

Tara Flynn is a Repeal campaigner, author, actor, playwright, comedian and columnist from Cork. Her books include *You're Grand: The Irishwoman's Secret Guide to Life* and *Giving Out Yards: The Art of the Complaint, Irish Style*.

19

STRANGE FRUIT

NELL McCAFFERTY

We need to have a conversation about conception, pregnancy and motherhood. After that, we need to talk about abortion.

The way I talked about both changed during the infamous and successful campaign of 1981–83 to introduce the Eighth Amendment into the constitution, which put the fertilised egg on a par with a pregnant woman.

As ever, the matter came up during a conversation in Derry with my mother, who was understandably upset by the 'pro-life' propaganda saying that abortion was, without qualification, the killing of an unborn child. 'No,' I explained, 'in the early stages of pregnancy, what is in the womb is a collection of cells that would not be visible under a microscope. That collection of cells could in no way be described as a baby,' I said confidently, and dismissively. (I was thirty-nine years old.)

My mother rose to her feet in the kitchen and said, 'Come you out here to the scullery with me.' We walked to the sink there, just opposite the gable wall in the backyard, to which blank canvas my mother was wont to stare in times of stress and confusion, her hands twisting the dishcloth. 'Do you see that oilcloth under my feet?' she asked, one hand on the sink, the other pointing to the floor under her feet. 'Are you telling me that the day I miscarried onto a newspaper on that exact spot, that I miscarried a bunch of cells? That was no bunch of cells, Nell. That was my baby, four months old.'

When the doctor arrived, he told her that it was the most perfect specimen of a miscarried baby that he had ever seen, and asked her permission to send it for preservation to a medical laboratory in Edinburgh. I asked what the specimen looked like and my mother replied, pointing to a framed Lowry picture, that it was like 'one of those stick people in that painting up on the wall.'

There was no Google in those days. It was not until 2017, at the pro-choice International Women's Day demonstration outside the Dáil that I saw a portrait on a banner of an early miscarriage. The banner was carried by pro-life counter-protestors. The foetus displayed was that of a 'murdered four-month-old baby in the womb', the protesters said. That was the first time that I had ever seen a replica of what my mother called the baby she had miscarried. Now I knew what she had been talking about, and what many other people had told me in the intervening years since 1983, of the miscarried babies they had buried in their own back gardens. 'What else could we do? We rang the doctor and he told us to just bury it in the garden. There probably dozens, maybe hundreds of miscarriages buried in back gardens all over Dublin.'

I had to think back to another tragedy experienced by my mother, revealed to me in one of the many conversations we had had since she first worried about my bringing back contraceptives on the Dublin–Belfast train journey of 1971 (when I was twenty-seven). She had just had a stroke, aged ninety, in the year 2000. When she recovered, she asked, 'Where is my baby buried?' She had given birth to a child in 1938, when she was twenty-eight. The baby died within minutes. Because there had been no time to send for the priest to baptise the girl baby, the child was deemed 'unsouled' by the Catholic Church, and there had been no formal ceremony or burial. My father had carried her in a cardboard shoebox up to the cemetery, after dark, and left her at the gate-lodge. Now my mother, fifty-two years later, wanted to know where her firstborn had been buried. In all the decades in between, during our weekly Sunday afternoon walks around the cemetery, Mary Ann had not been mentioned. My mother taught us to read by having us recite what was on the headstones. There was nothing else to do in Protestant-controlled and ruled Derry, gloomy Sunday Sabbath coming down.

When Mammy asked, with wrenching despair and loss, where was the body of her firstborn, my super-efficient sister Nuala found the receipt from the cemetery officials, and went to the directed location. She found an unmarked mass grave in an overgrown abandoned stretch of waste ground. Nuala went straight to the Catholic Bishop of Derry – the Bloody Sunday priest Edward Daly – and asked him about such treatment of babies in a time when the pro-lifers were erecting 'angel plots' for such fruits of the womb all over Ireland. Within a week, the bishop had the waste ground landscaped and an angel row dedicated. A priest picked a random spot and said that Mary Ann had been buried there. We bought a red marble headstone wrought in the shape of a shoebox, and the priest gave Mary Ann a formal blessing and farewell. My mother was there. Afterwards, she wept to me that Mary Ann was not in heaven as the priest had declared and, reciting Catholic doctrine, said, 'She was never baptised. She will be in Limbo for ever. She will never get into Heaven.' My mother died in 2004, before the Catholic Church pronounced that the status of Limbo is actually in limbo, and that the Church had not made up its mind on this cruel theological matter.

Years before she died, my mother told me that in the event of one of her granddaughters being raped and impregnated, she, my mother, would go personally to Rome and ask the Pope for permission to have the raped fruit of the womb aborted. She sighed and fell silent when I pointed out the utter impossibility of that. There were some matters beyond discussion when a wordy daughter such as myself brought reason relentlessly to bear. I could practically hear her brain clicking in the silence, though. My mother had reluctantly come to the acceptance of the necessity of abortion in some cases. On many such matters, over the years, as one broken marriage after another, for example, rolled into the house, my mother visibly wished that I would just shut up and let her think her way through things. 'It's like Southfork in here,' she said, wistfully referencing the soap opera *Dallas* as yet another challenge in a changing family presented itself. Then she'd chuckle and I'd be banished.

The worst and best day was when the doctor advised that we send for the priest because my ninety-three-year-old mother was definitely dying. The priest came and was gone within minutes of giving Extreme Unction. My mother was furious afterwards. 'That priest took one look at me in the bed and said, "Ah sure, an old woman like you has no sins, Mrs McCafferty." He knows nothing. He's a boy. I want a man.'

I went dutifully to the cathedral and Bishop Daly came over immediately. He and my mother were alone together for two hours and more, as he heard her last confession. When he came out for a cup of tea, I asked Daly, 'Were you man enough for her?' He grinned and said, 'She ran rings round me, Nell.' The bishop's brother had, a week previously, left his wife for another and younger woman. 'Who confessed to whom?' I asked. 'That's our business, and you'll never know,' he replied.

My mother, when I brought her in the tea, grinned and sighed in discreet, silent satisfaction.

I don't have those kinds of conversations or understandings any more. The International Women's day demos, 8 March 2017, calling for the repeal of the Eighth, illustrate the point definitively. The first demo on O'Connell Street bridge had a young woman holding aloft a placard that declared: *If I wanted the government in my womb, I'd fuck a Senator.* I pointed out officiously that she surely meant a male senator, and was told to 'fuck off'. Another placard declared: *Get the constitution out of my cuntstitution.* When a photographer pointed out that her newspaper would not, could not, print such language, she was told to 'fuck off'.

Later that evening, in the pitch dark, thousands of supportive people were addressed from the sidewalk, by means of a hand-held loudhailer, and we could neither hear nor see. I looked at the purported picture banner of an aborted four-month-old foetus, and was told by pro-lifers that I supported murder.

We need to talk, sisters and brothers. 'Fuck' and 'cunt' do not comprise conversation, and if that does not change, we will not get the complete range of abortion rights that are a female's right to choose. We need to talk about Enda Kenny's legacy to Ireland; the highest rate of homelessness known since the famine. There is no room at the inn for nurturing the fruit of our wombs. Modern family life dictates a two-income, mother-father combination of paid working careers, with the newborn dropped off at the crèche when only months old.

We need to talk indoors, not shout outdoors. No conversation about abortion is complete without celebration, in the context of contraception, of the magnificent plenitude of conception, pregnancy and motherhood. The thrust of current feminist shouts, particularly from the young, is almost exclusively about abortion, abortion and abortion, to the exclusion of almost all else. The difficulties of modern parenting must surely be addressed in the current housing crisis, with crippling mortgage and rental, and costly crèche difficulties. Abortion is the last resort, not the first, of womanhood.

Nell McCafferty was a founder member of the Irish Women's Liberation Movement, 1970.

20

THE US'S
UNA MULLALLY

Down the docks
Raves and apartment blocks
The fruit machines and slots
On boats named after poets
The Us's are boarding

On the Air Coach from Cork
Or the Go Bus from Galway
Or at Limerick Junction wondering if snaiceanna is really
    an Irish word
The Us's are travelling

On their way
To get abortions
The Us's

Right now, there's a couple in Dublin airport
Wheelie case and Xanax
Going back to his ma's gaff
The biscuit breaking off in the cup of tea

Her favourite mug
It says Fair City
She won it in a competition on RTÉ

Done with shame
Finished with guilt
Goes to bed
Electric blanket
And the continental quilt
The Us's

In Malahide today
A Citizen's Assembly
Voting for bodily autonomy
Saying Ireland is a pro-choice country
The Us's

We're constantly being told by politicians about 'middle Ireland'
Polling and tolling mysterious conservative bells
Resistant to change
Scared of progress
Here. Dáil Eireann, stop describing yourselves

I'm
Saint Vincent appalled
By responsibility dodging in the Dáil
It's over, no more, no way
Because, well, what are nuns doing with multimillion property
portfolios anyway

Tonight, we are the Us's

We are the black jumpers and fist bumpers
The marching drum thumpers
The megaphone wielders
The friends and families who won't wait
Who shout
Not the Church not the State
Women must decide their fate
The Us's

We are middle Ireland
We are the coasts
We are the cities, the villages, its children, its ghosts
We are the grannies, and farmers, and students
We're on the dole
We're earning loads
We're scraping our rent together
We should've never taken out that loan
We're married, we're divorced
We're up again in the courts
We're late for school
We're early to rise
Walking fields
Opening the shop
Planning the wedding
We're regretting last night's shots
We're at the gym and in the boozer
We don't know why the dog's scared of the hoover
The Us's

We are *Young Offenders*
We're Adams and Pauls
We don't have a breeze what's going on in the Dáil

We slept with the wrong person
We wrote Bobby Sands on a toilet door
We're caring for our parents
We're wondering what she's looking at me for
We're on the guest list
We're not getting in
We keep our few bob in a USA biscuit tin
We've got tea on the range
A booster seat in the Range Rover
We're sleeping in doorways
We're raging *The Good Wife* is over
The Us's

We're training year round
We just started yoga
We're getting Dine in for Two
We got a class selfie at the Cliffs of Moher
The Us's

We're in bits 'cos our best pal killed himself
We're on Tinder worrying we'll be left on the shelf
We're up at dawn making Christmas cake
We're giving out about Snapchat fakes
We're in the petrol station glancing at the papers
We're in a wetsuit at Grand Canal Dock
We're in Coppers wondering if there are any takers
We're selling hats, scarves and headbands
We're working out our Australia plans
We need to get the roof fixed
We're on a hospital waiting list
We're going to find out which neighbour's dog keeps
    shitting outside the door

THE US'S

We're at our daughter's Holy Communion wondering what
   we're crying for
We're at a parent–teacher meeting
We bought off the plans
We're down the canal with a bag of cans
The Us's

We need a new laptop
We're getting our nails done
We want Wenger out
We wish daft.ie had a comment section
We're sick and tired of the Luas works
We had our bike nicked
The strike was on so we walked to work
The Us's

We're pucking sliotars
We're buying Rihanna's Puma slippers
We're at the Ploughing
We're writing code
We've just discovered a potato wedge roll
We're going home locked and listening to 'A Woman's Heart'
We are in the change about to start
We're rolling pinners
We're biting quarters
We're yer ma
Yer man
Yer wan
Your daughter
The Us's

We're here
On cobblestones made smooth from marching
Knowing what kind of republic we want to be
Jaded from smoking-section bants and debates on TV3
And if you're angry that's OK
Use it
Channel it
Get your canvassing boots ready
The Us's

The Us's will
Do away with Direct Provision
Dismantle poverty
The Us's know that gay marriage doesn't matter unless it's part of
broader social change
The Us's aren't afraid

We'll have the barneys
And from that rubble
Build a shelter we can all stand under
The Us's

We are the Goonies in the well
Saying this one right here, this was my dream
Know that it will come true
Don't doubt that just a few can change the world
It's the only thing that ever has
But it won't just be a couple of campaigners who'll see
this through
It's you, your mam, your dad
the Us's

Because what you're feeling tonight
When you look around
Is when you realise so many strangers are on your side
The Us's

We'll be in Dublin Castle
On another sunny day
Screaming go on Ireland
Go on the Us's
This is our time, tonight, today.

Una Mullally is a writer from Dublin. She is a journalist with the *Irish Times*, and her writing has also featured in *Granta*, the *Guardian* and several anthologies. She is the author of the Irish marriage-equality oral history *In the Name of Love*.

CREDITS

Sara Falkensjo's personal story, interview by Rosita Boland, in an extract from an *Irish Times* article on the X-ile Project, Friday 20 May 2017, republished with permission.

Lucy Watmough's personal story, in conversation with Bárbara A. Soares, originally published in *The Circular*. Reprinted with permission.

'Laundry' by Mary Coll first appeared in her collection *Silver* published by Arlen House 2017.

'History Lesson' originally appeared in Elaine Feeney's collection *Rise*, published by Salmon Poetry.

'I don't know what I thought abortion would be like' is from *How to Be a Woman* by Caitlin Moran. Published by Ebury Press. Reprinted by permission of The Random House Group © 2011.

'We Marched, and We Will March Again' by Louise O'Neill, a version of this piece originally appeared in the *Irish Examiner*.

'Kelly's Story' by Mark O'Halloran is an extract from his screenplay, *Life*.

'Heartbreak' by Emmet Kirwan was commissioned and developed with THISISPOPBABY for the theatre production RIOT, Winner of Best Production at Dublin Fringe 2016.

ACKNOWLEDGEMENTS

Thank you to all of those who funded this book by pledging donations on unbound.com. You are the reason it exists.

To the amazing team at Unbound who conceived of, developed and published this anthology, as well as managed the crowdfunding campaign. Thank you to Phil Connor for the idea, enthusiasm and trust. Thank you to Imogen Denny who steered the project through to fruition and who has the patience of a saint. Thank you to Mark Ecob who designed the book jacket, thanks also to Georgia Odd, Lauren Fulbright, Amy Winchester and Kate Quarry.

A massive thank you to all of the contributors for their amazing and considered contributions, Jill & Gill, Maser, Uterus Prime aka Rae Moore, Hannah Hogan and Adam Hurley, Niall Sweeney, Love & Robots, Isleen Design, Roisin Agnew, Aoife Dooley, Alice Maher, Jessica Saunders, Andrea Horan, Sarah Fox, Will St Leger, Lucy Watmough, Sara Falkensjo, Helen Linehan, the women who shared their stories anonymously, Mary Coll, Anne Enright, Aisling Bea, Kitty Holland, Elaine Feeney, Caitlin Moran, Sinéad Gleeson, Colm O'Gorman, Sarah Maria Griffin, Louise O'Neill, Mark O'Halloran, Ailbhe Smyth, Lisa McInerney, Siobhán Fenton, Emmet Kirwan, Ellie Kisyombe, Tara Flynn, Nell McCafferty, Kiki Na Art, Alison Laredo, and anyone else who contributed to what features here across writing, design, photography and any other aspect of it.

An extra thank you to Louise O'Neill who pointed Unbound in my direction, and to Sinéad Gleeson for her advice and suggestions. Thank you to Anna Cosgrave who graciously collaborated on the limited edition cover design.

Thank you to the Abortion Rights Campaign, the Coalition to Repeal the Eighth Amendment, the Artists Campaign to Repeal the Eighth Amendment, Amnesty International Ireland, all of the ancillary, local and solidarity campaigns around the movements for reproductive rights in Ireland and to repeal the Eighth Amendment, the Abortion Support Network, the Repeal Project, Strike4Repeal, the HunReal Issues, the X-ile Project, ROSA, the organisations, grassroots groups and individuals who are campaigning in ways big and small for reproductive rights in Ireland, and all the people and groups who have done so in the past.

Thank you to those on the frontline of this issue: campaigners, medical professionals, activists, lawyers, pro-choice politicians, and others in clinics, organisations and support networks. Thank you to those people who supply abortion pills to women in Ireland. Thank you to those who are writing about this issue or making art about this issue. Thank you to those who donate to the cause of reproductive rights in Ireland and who fundraise for it. Thank you to the women who share their abortion stories and fight for their rights in courts.

Thank you to my editors at the *Irish Times* for their patience while I was busy with this anthology, especially Rachel Collins, Laurence Mackin and John McManus.

Thank you to my agent, Emma Paterson, at Rogers, Coleridge & White for her patience. Thank you to Catherine Conroy for the 'Daft' line.

Thank you to The Birds; Meadzer, Lainey, Ro and Izzy for your counsel and friendship. Thank you to my friends and family for your support and for putting up with me when I can't hang out because I'm writing.

Thank you especially to Sarah Francis who steers and guides me through everything.

SUPPORTERS

Unbound is a new kind of publishing house. Our books are funded directly by readers. This was a very popular idea during the late eighteenth and early nineteenth centuries. Now we have revived it for the internet age. It allows authors to write the books they really want to write and readers to support the writing they would most like to see published.

The names listed below are of readers who have pledged their support and made this book happen. If you'd like to join them, visit: www.unbound.co.uk.

AC
Louise Acheson
Tegan Alana
Emma Allen
Ioanna Anderson
Caoileann Appleby
Clare Archibald
Richard Ashcroft
Sandra Austin
Ali B
Francesca B.
Banshee Literary Journal
John Barker
Brian Barnes
Michael Nanci Barron
Aisling Bea
Aine Beamish
Helen Beaumont
Lian Bell
Suzie Bennett
Ciara Bergin
Claire Bird
Eloise Birnam-Wood
Robbie Blake

Blanaid's Hennessy
Ailie Blunnie
Gilyana Borlikova
Lynn Boylan MEP
Claire Bradley
Louise Brady
Deirdre Breen
Eleanor Brooks
Elaine Buckley
Mary Buckley
Nell Buckley
Christine Burns
John Butler
Anita Byrne
Cian Byrne
Conor Byrne
Karen Byrne
Lena Byrne
Neil Byrne
Niall Byrne
Suzy Byrne
Tríona Byrne
Ruth Caden
Michael Cahill

Kai Caimo
Sophie Cameron
Fidelma Carolan
Margo Carr
Eoghan Carrick
Maeve Carroll
Sally Carty
Anto Casey
Emma Cassidy
Elise Catteau
Mélissa Chouikrat
Joseph Clarke
Malachy Clerkin
Declan Clifford
Karina Clifford
Denis Clohessy
Maggie Collins
Rachel Collins
Katherine Condon
Nial Conlan
Rachel Conlon
Lisa Connell
Charlie Connelly
Aisling Considine
Kerryann Conway
Morgan Cooke
Eoin Cooney
Breda Corish @N16Breda
Charlotte Cousins
Tom Creed
Sophie Cremen
Lucie Crichlow
Michael Croke
Maggie Cronin
Muireann Crowley
Marion Crtr
Helen Cullen
Sarah Cullen
Senan Cullinan
Shane Culloty
Fiona Cunningham
Mark Curran

Victoria Curtis
Abi Daly
Gráinne Daly
Laura Daly Brogan
Fionn Davenport
Jennifer Davidson
Matt Davies
Sarah Davis-Goff
Becca Day-Preston
Aoife de Burca
Cassie Delaney
Dee Delany
Clare Delargy
Rebecca Dickson
W Dinan
Bernie Divilly
Carolanne Doherty
Sonya Donnelly
Mark Donoghue
Katie Donovan
Angela Dorgan
Sarah Dowd
Rebecca Dowling
Darragh Doyle
Diarmuid Doyle
Jean Doyle
Barry Du Monde
The Dublin Well Woman Centre
Aoife Duffy
Jenny Duffy
Ciaran Duggan
Irina Dzhambazova
Eva Early
Ken Early
Elaine Edwards
Emma El-Sahn
Eimear Ellis
Mairead Enright
Mick Ers
Chloe Fagan
Charlotte Featherstone
Aislinn Fell

Gavin Fitzgerald
Geraldine Fitzgerald
Brenda Fitzsimons
Colm Flaherty
Emma Flanagan
Ciara Flood
Aoife Flynn
Rebecca Flynn
Tara Flynn
Tony Flynn
Julie Fogarty
Siobhán Foran
Kathryn Foskin
Olwen Fouéré
Sarah Fox
Helen Francis
Padraig Francis
Sarah Francis
Ben Fraser
Lisa Gallagher
Mary Gallagher
Brian Gallwey
Claire Galvin
Majda Gama
Colm Garvey
Martin Gaughan
Dolores Gibbons
Jack Gibson
Brynne Gilmore
Thyrza Ging
Rory Gleeson
A Glynn
Susie Glynn
Róise Goan
Nicky Gogan
Gillian Eva Golden
Deirdre M Gorman
Li Gri
Peter Hall
Jessica Halligan
Niamh Hamill
Leanne Harte

Dylan Haskins
Ella Hassett
Isabel Hayes
Jenny Headen
Caroline B. Heafey
Grainne Healy
Karen Healy
Benjamin Hemmens
Claire Hennessy
Lorraine Hester
Clodagh Higgins
Maeve Higgins
Zoe Holden
Katie Holly
Antonia Honeywell
Naomi Hooban
Andrea Horan
Conor Horgan
Abbie Horrigan
Elisa Duncan Cullen & Orla Hubbard
Edel Hughes
Andrew Hyland
Roisin Ingle
Rob Ivory
Jennifer Jennings
Danniella Josephine
Malgorzata Kalek
Gillian Kane
Lois Kapila
Aaron Kavanagh
Lizzie Kaye
Lynda Kealy
Charles Keane
Heather Keane
Gerry Kearns
Wayne Kearns
Emma Keaveney
Julie Kelleher
Margaret Kelleher
Aoife Kelly
Carolyn Kelly
Clare Kelly

Philip Kelly
Alice Kennelly
David Kennelly
Katie Kent
Jackie Kerr
Tasha Kerry
Gemma Keyes
Marian Keyes
Alannah Kidney
Eoghan Kidney
Etain Kidney
Fionn Kidney
Dan Kieran
Molly King
Mary Knox O'Brien
Ian Lambkin
Gavin Lavelle
Lauren Lawler
Tom Lawlor
Anneka Lawson
Sinead Leavy
Sadhbh Lee
Patrick Leech
Jerry Lehane
Hilary Lennon
Sharon Lennon
John Leo
Sandra Lewis
Bernie & Katherine Linnane McBride
Fátima del Carmen López Sevilla
Elizabeth Loughnane
Sarah Lynch
Sarah M
Liosa Mac
Fiach Mac Conghail
Brona Mac Entee
Colm MacCárthaigh
Laurence Mackin
Dermot Magee
Grainne Maguire
Elaine Mai
Ailbhe Malone

Fifi Marbhán
Charlotte Marie
Nathalie Marquez Courtney
Henry Martin
Al Maser
Matt Matheson
Breda Mayock
Sheena McAfee
Nora-Ide McAuliffe
Eimear McBride
Fiona McCann
Kate McCarthy
Steven McCarthy
Siobhan McClelland
Meghan McCusker
Michael McDermott
Jeanie McDonald
Collette McEntee
Roisin McGann
Simon McGarr
Aisling McGee
Kevin McGee
Noel McGee
Elizabeth McGeown
Sharon McGlone
Rhonda McGovern
Roisín McGuigan
Sharon McGuigan
Oisín McKenna
Belinda McKeon
Una McKevitt
Sarah McKibben
Ciaran McKinney
Paul Mcloughlin
Philly McMahon
Alan McMonagle
Dominique McMullan
Dervla Mcneice
Kieran McNulty
Louise McSharry
Anthea McTeirnan
Laura McVeigh

Marie Therese McWalter
Bairbre Meade
Helen Meaney
Cerys Millward
Brendan Minish
John Mitchinson
Lucy Moffatt
Deirdre Molloy
Christine Monk
Daniel Morrison
Barbara Morrissey
Bush Moukarzel
Niall Muckian
Meg Mulcahy
Aoife Mullally
Deirdre Mullally
John Mullally
Patricia Mullally
Barry Mullarkey
Sinead Mullins
Aoife Murphy
Celina Murphy
Cian Murphy
Emer Murphy
Paul Murphy
Ruth Murphy
Catherine Murray
Mary Nally
Carlo Navato
McKinley Neal
Annemarie Neary
Louise Neill
Stephen Neill (PaddyAnglican)
Kris Nelson
Ruairí Newman
Aifric Ní Chríodáin
Dearbhla Ní Cuinn
Louise Ní Fhiannachta
Mary Ni Lochlainn
Sarah Ní Mháirtín
Zoe Ni Riordain
Niamh NicGhabhann

Brian Nisbet
Sharon Nolan
Sinéad Nolan
Amica Sciortino Nowlan
Liz Nugent
Sinead Nugent
Osgur Ó Ciardha
Seana O Rodaigh
Sinead O Shea
Cian O'Brien
Ciarán Sarky O'Brien
Kate O'Brien
Laura O'Brien
Lauren O'Brien
Liana O'Cleirigh
Claire O'Connell
Hugh O'Conor
Roisin O'Dea
Annie O'Doherty
David O'Doherty
Fionntán O'Donnell
Katherine O'Donnell
Patrick O'Donoghue
Caroline O'Dowd
Enda O'Dowd
Ita O'Driscoll
Ken O'Duffy
Colm O'Gorman
Mark O'Halloran
Daithi O'Laoghaire
Elaine O'Meara
Mark O'Neill
Martha O'Neill
Beth O'Rafferty
Sara O'Sullivan
Shane O'Sullivan
Emer O'Toole
Fintan O'Toole
Hazel O'Toole
Cassie Oakman
Dan Oggly
Sarah Parker

Ruth Patten
Éadaoin Patton
Kerry Payne
Julie Pichon
Rosie Plunkett
Justin Pollard
Helen Porter
Aine Power
Aisling Prior
Elaine Prunty
Tricia Purcell
Claire Pyke
Ciarán Quigley
Aideen Quilty
Síobhra Quinlan
Hannah Quinn
Natalie Radmall-Quirke
Lynn Rafferty
John Regan and Deepali Patel
Trish Reilly
Aoife Riach
Senta Rich
Amy Roberts
Anna Rodgers
Matilda Romaine
Eabha Rosenstock
Ann Ryan
Jennifer Ryan
Meadhbh Ryan
Philippa Ryder
Elena Schmitz
Ruth Seavers
Bill Shipsey
Eithne Shortall
Shireen Shortt

Jan Shúilleabháin
Lorna Sixsmith
Alissa Skinner
Gerard Smith
Rachael Prendergast Spollen
Will St Leger
Rebecca Stacey
Claire Sumner
Keith Sutherland
Aoife Courtney Swan
Female Szagala
Conleth Teevan
Carla Teixeira
Shirley Temple Bar
Sarah Thin
Maria Tivnan
Karl Tooher
Mary Traynor
Orla Vaughan
Sally Vince
Mark Walker
Alice Walsh
Amy Walsh
Brian and Emma Walsh
Cathy Walsh
Samuel Walsh
Sharon Watters
Paul Webster
Louise White
Willie White
Andrea Wilkinson
Karen Williams
Sarah Wilson
JA Young